WOMEN, ART AND GEOMETRY IN SOUTHERN AFRICA

WOMEN, ART

AND GEOMETRY

IN SOUTHERN AFRICA

PAULUS GERDES

Africa World Press, Inc.

P.O. Box 1892

Trenton, NJ 08607

P.O. Box 48

Asmara, ERITREA

Africa World Press, Inc.

P.O. Box 1892
Trenton, NJ 08607

P.O. Box 48
Asmara, ERITREA

Book and Cover design: Jonathan Gullery

This book is set in Veljovic Book and Nueva

Library of Congress Cataloging-in-Publication Data

Gerdes, Paulus.
    Women, art and geometry in Southern Africa / by Paulus Gerdes.
       p.   cm.
    Includes bibliographical references (p.).
    ISBN 0-86543-601-0 (hb). --ISBN 0-86543-602-9 (pb)
       1. Handicraft--Africa, Southern. 2. Decoration and ornament--Africa, Southern. 3. Ethnomathematics--Africa, Southern.
    4. Geometry in art. 5. Women artisans--Africa, Southern.
    I. Title.
    TT119.S64G47 1998
    745.4'4968--dc21   98-21977
                                   CIP

CONTENTS

Preface

African peoples and countries in general, and those in Southern Africa entering the post-apartheid era in particular, are facing the urgent need to awaken and nurture their magnificent potential for the benefit of all.

Women, constituting half of the population, are still strongly under-represented in scientific and technological careers where mathematical ideas play an important role. For instance, only 20% of the mathematicians and mathematics educators included in the "*Who is Who in Mathematics and Mathematics Education in Southern Africa*" (Gerdes ed., 1992, 1993) are women. Lydia Makhubu, chemist and Vice-Chancellor of the University of Swaziland, points out that in addition to other sociocultural obstacles, women themselves appear to lack the confidence to take up studies in the science fields that have—in the context of school traditions transplanted from Europe to Africa—been considered male domains (cf. Makhubu, 1991, p. 143). Outside the context of the forcibly imported school, however, Southern African women have traditionally been involved in cultural activities—such as ceramics, beading, mural decoration, basket weaving, hair braiding, tattooing, string figures—which bear a strong artistic and mathematical character. Although the mathematical aspects of these traditional cultural activities have so far not, or hardly, been recognised by 'Academia', this does not render them less mathematical.

After all, what is mathematics all about?

The famous number theorist, Hardy, once wrote that "A mathematician, like a painter or a poet, is a maker of patterns. If his patterns are more permanent than theirs, it is because they are made with *ideas*." and "The mathematician's patterns, like the painter's or the poet's, must be *beautiful*. The ideas, like the colours or the words, must fit together in a harmonious way. Beauty is the first test: there is no permanent place in the world for ugly mathematics" (Hardy, 1940, p. 84, 85). Along the same lines go the remarks of the Cameroonean mathematician Njock: "Pure mathematics is the art of creating and imaginating. In this sense black art is mathematics" (Njock, 1985, p. 8). Southern African women have created and continue to create, invent, and imaginate beautiful patterns.

The main objective of the book *Women, Art and Geometry in Southern Africa* is to call attention to some mathematical aspects and ideas incorporated in the patterns invented by women in Southern Africa. It is our wish to contribute to the valuing, revival and development of traditions which may otherwise vanish.

In an earlier book *"Sipatsi: Technology, Art and Geometry in Inhambane"* (1994) it was first explained which mathematical ideas are involved in the weaving of sipatsi handbags by Gitonga speaking women in the Mozambican province of Inhambane. Then a catalogue of strip patterns with which the basketweavers decorate their *sipatsi* was presented, followed by examples of an educational and mathematical exploration of these handbags. With the publication of *Women, Art and Geometry in Southern Africa* it is hoped to stimulate research all over the region, such as that which led to *"Sipatsi: Technology, Art and Geometry in Inhambane"*: fieldwork, pattern gathering and analysis, and educational experimentation.

The suggestions presented in this book attempt to support the preparation of further initiatives which may contribute to a fuller realization of the mathematical potential of women (and men) in Southern Africa, and to—what Africa so urgently needs, in the words of the well-known historian Ki-Zerbo—a "new educational system, properly rooted in both society and environment, and therefore apt to generate the self-confidence from which imagination springs " (Ki-Zerbo, 1990, p.104). Several of the suggestions were briefly presented earlier at conferences and talks in Swaziland (University of Swaziland, Kwaluseni, 1992; Waterford College, Mbabane, 1993), Lesotho (SAMSA Symposium, Maseru, 1986; National University of Lesotho, 1980, 1995), Botswana (SAMSA Symposium, Gaborone, 1993), South Africa (AMESA-lectures in Durban, Cape Town, Johannesburg, 1994).

Women, Art and Geometry in Southern Africa is dedicated to all the artists, artisans and geometers who create the fascinating worlds of sipatsi, titja, mafielo, oku-taleka, nembo, ovilame, litema, ikghuptu, ...

Maputo, March 27, 1995
Paulus Gerdes
Universidade Pedagógica
C.P. g15, Maputo, Mozambique

The first edition of Women, Art and Geometry in Southern Africa was published in 1995 by Mozambique's 'Universidade Pedagógica'.

In this new edition by Africa World Press, the book is extended with an appendix (an initial response to a challenge made in the first edition) written by Salimo Saide, one of my former students at the 'Universidade Pedagógica'. He presents extracts of interviews with some of the old and maybe last female potters from the Yao speaking population and describes some geometrical aspects of their pottery decoration. The Yao live in Mozambique's northern Nyassa Province, that borders Lake Nyassa and Tanzania.

I dedicate the new edition by Africa World Press to my youngest daughter Likilisa.

June 1998
Paulus Gerdes

Acknowledgements

My thanks go to my colleagues Abdulcarimo Ismael, Abílio Mapapá and Marcos Cherinda (Mathematics Department, Universidade Pedagógica [UP]), and Eduardo Medeiros (Department of Cultural Anthropology, UP) for their comments on the first draft of several chapters of this book; to Eduardo Medeiros for his kind permission to have access to his dossier on tattooings in Mozambique; to Jill Gerrish (Department of English, UP) for the linguistic revision; to Ângelo Maduela (Computer Services, UP) for his computer maintenance; to my staff Salima Give, Ângela Muthimba and Teresa Jamal-Dine (Office of the Rector, UP) for their support; to Marcos Cherinda for taking photographs of baskets and brooms in the author's collection. I acknowledge the financial support of the Swedish Agency for Research Cooperation with Developing Countries (SAREC) to Mozanbique's Ethnomathematics Research Project. I am very grateful for the interest many colleagues, students and friends have shown in the preparation of this book. Above all, I thank my wife Marcela Libombo and my daughter Lesira for their encouragement.

I thank Aarnout Brombacher for the linguistic revision and comments on the Appendix by Salimo Saide, included in the new edition.

1. SIPATSI—
WOVEN HANDBAGS

Because of their beauty and utility, straw woven handbags called *sipatsi* (singular: *gipatsi*) in Gitonga, a language spoken in Inhambane Province, are among the products of Mozambican basketry best loved by locals and foreign visitors alike. The making of *sipatsi* is practised nowadays by both men and women, having been formerly exclusively a women's activity. Photographs 1.1 and 1.2 display *sipatsi*.

Photograph 1.1

Photograph 1.2

For a number of years, I have systematically collected *sipatsi*, selected for their decorative motifs. The collection that I have established so far shows the existence of more than one hundred different motifs, which reveals the force of imagination and the artistic and geometric creativity of the basket weavers who make them.

In workshops with students and lecturers at Mozambique's *Universidade Pedagógica* (UP), on the theme of ethnomathematics — the analysis of mathematics and mathematics education in their cultural context — I presented *sipatsi*, along with other cultural elements of Mozambique. One of the students, Gildo Bulafo, a native speaker of Gitonga, became particularly interested in *sipatsi*. During June and July 1993, in order to know more about the production of the *sipatsi*, he conducted his first field trip to interview basket weavers in Inhambane Province.

In the first chapter of our book *Sipatsi: Technology, Art and Geometry in Inhambane*, Gildo Bulafo reports on his fieldwork, revealing the knowledge of the basket weavers. In the second chapter, I present a catalogue of strip patterns with which basket weavers decorate *sipatsi*. The patterns in this catalogue may serve as a source of inspiration for architects, painters, and other artists; they could be reproduced on clothes, walls, stamps, etc.

One objective of ethnomathematical research consists of looking for possibilities of improving the teaching of mathematics by embedding it into the cultural context of pupils and teachers. A type of mathematics education which succeeds in valuing the scientific knowledge inherent in the culture by using this knowledge to lay the foundations for providing quicker and better access to the scientific heritage of the whole of humanity, is desirable. It is in this sense that in the third chapter of *Sipatsi: Technology, Art and Geometry in Inhambane* some suggestions are made for an educational and mathematical use of *sipatsi*.

In this first chapter of *Women, Art and Geometry in Southern Africa*, a short introduction to the making and use of *sipatsi* will be presented.

Figure 1.1 gives examples (of parts) of strip patterns with which the basket weavers decorate their *sipatsi*. [1]

Figure 1.1

When weaving their *sipatsi*, the basket-makers repeat their decorative motif in an oblique or diagonal position, as Figure 1.2 illustrates for the strip pattern in Figure 1.3. In this example, to generate one copy of the motif, 8 coloured strands are needed. We may say that the motif has 8 as its *period*.

Figure 1.2

Figure 1.3

One of the conditions that a *gipatsi* must satisfy to be considered beautiful and of good quality is the following: in each ornamental strip, the motif must fit exactly a whole number of times around the *gipatsi*. This implies that the total number of coloured strands has to be a common multiple of each of the periods of the motifs used for its decoration. For instance, in the example shown in Figure 1.4, the total number of coloured strands has to be a multiple of 10 and 3.

For technical reasons related to the weaving process, the number of coloured strands must also always be a multiple of 4. So the basket weavers have to determine (mentally) the common multiple of 4 and of each of the periods of the motifs they have chosen before weaving their *sipatsi*. Since the common multiple is sometimes too big to produce a *gipatsi* of an acceptable size, the weavers look for the best *approximate* solution within the acceptable boundaries.

Figure 1.4

Analysis of the symmetries the strip patterns on *sipatsi* display constitutes an interesting educational theme. I have used it in classes with future mathematics teachers. For example, the strip patterns in Figures 1.1 and 1.3 have horizontal and/or vertical axes of symmetry. The strip pattern shown in Figure 1.5 does not have any axis of symmetry, but displays the property of being invariant under a half turn. In other words, there exist points (marked black and white in the illustration) such that the pattern does not alter when rotated, in the plane of the drawing, through a straight angle about these points.

Figure 1.5

Figure 1.6a shows a strip pattern with other properties (cf. the upper part of Figure 1.4). It has a peculiar symmetry.

Figure 1.6.a

Figure 1.6.b

When one reflects the pattern about its horizontal axis, as indicated in Figure 1.6b, one obtains the pattern illustrated in Figure 1.7, which appears rather similar to the initial pattern. If one then translates this last pattern to the left (or right) a distance equal to half the distance between two corresponding points of two adjacent copies of the decorative motif, one returns to the original (infinite) strip pattern. In this case, one says that the pattern of Figure 1.7 remains invariant under a glide reflection (or under a translated reflection).

Figure 1.8

On the basis of their (different) symmetries, strip patterns may be classified. From a theoretical algebraic point of view, seven such classes, seven infinite "one-dimensional" symmetry groups exist (see

7

Figure 1.9

Appendix 1). In other words, there are seven essentially distinct ways to repeat a motif on a strip. The creativity of the *sipatsi* weavers also expresses itself in the fact that they invented strip patterns belonging to all seven different theoretically possible symmetry groups.

Once I had used *sipatsi* as an introduction to the analysis and classification of strip patterns for my students, they started to apply their newly-developed ideas in other contexts. For example, they analysed tyre profiles (see Figure 1.9): To which symmetry classes do these (and other) profiles belong? Must tyre profiles necessarily have certain types of symmetries? Why? What are the advantages?

8

Figure 1.10

The geometry of ornamentation of *sipatsi* raises many interesting questions for investigation. For example, how many ornamental strip patterns of the *gipatsi* type exist, of given dimensions *p* and *d*, where *p* denotes the period and *d* the diagonal height of the decorative motif? In the case where the dimensions are 2x4, six different strip patterns of the *gipatsi* type exist. Figure 1.10 illustrates these strip patterns, together with the motifs that generate them.

There are many possibilities for the mathematical and educational use of *sipatsi*, contributing to the improvement of mathematics teaching by embedding it into the cultural context of pupils and teachers. The confidence of young people, in particular that of girls, in their mathematical capacities and potential may increase as they examine the mathematics of *sipatsi*.

9

NOTES

1. When one speaks about strip pat-
    terns, one imagines them infinite
    in the sense that the decorative
    motif may be repeated, at fixed dis-
    tances, endlessly to the left and to
    the right.

TITJA—COILED BASKETS

Colourful basket bowls are woven by women in Swaziland. The technique they use is a type of coiling. Sisal thread *umtiye* is handspun around a grass coil into a basket, called *sitja* (plural: *titja*). Figure 2.1 shows the outlines of typical *titja*, and Figure 2.2 a coil.

Outlines of *titja*
Figure 2.1

Figure 2.3 shows how successive circuits of the coil are bound closely together by the thread stitches. Changes of colour in the decoration of the basket are achieved by using threads of different colours.

A coil
Figure 2.2

Figure 2.4 shows a Swazi basket-bowl in the author's collection seen from above. It displays a fivefold symmetry, that is, its motif (see Figure 2.5) appears in five distinct positions which are *regularly* distributed around its centre: Rotating counterclockwise the motif (position [1]) through a fifth of a complete turn (in other words, through an angle of $(\frac{360^{\circ}}{5})$ or 72°) around the centre, one obtains the next position [2], etc. After five such rotations, the motif returnes to its initial position: the sixth position is the same as the first position, or, [6] = [1].

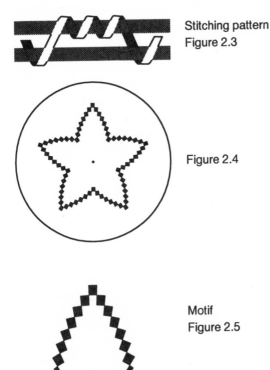

Stitching pattern
Figure 2.3

Figure 2.4

Motif
Figure 2.5

Five distinct positions
Figure 2.6

At the same time, the decoration of the aforementioned basket-bowl has axial (or bilateral) symmetry. In fact, there are five symmetry axes (see Figure 2.7).

In the mathematical study of (finite) designs, it is said that the decorative design of the basket-bowl in Figure 2.4 belongs to type $d5$. The 5 stands for fivefold rotational symmetry and the d for "dihedral," indicating that the design also has reflection symmetry. In general, the designs of type dn have reflection symmetry as well as n-fold rotational symmetry.

Five symmetry axes
Figure 2.7

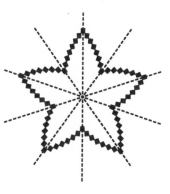

Figure 2.8 displays a basket-bowl with a design that belongs to type $d4$.

The weavers of *titja* prefer to produce baskets of the type dn. Of the 25 *titja* in the author's collection, 22 are of the type dn. Several of them are reproduced in Plate 2.a–e.

Figure 2.8

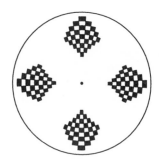

Three basket-bowls in the author's collection do not have a mirror symmetry. Figure 2.9 shows one of them. It displays only (10-fold) rotational symmetry. One says it has the type $c10$, where c stands for "cyclic". Its motif appears in ten distinct positions.

From one position to the next, one has to rotate the motif through one tenth of a complete turn, that is through an angle of $(\frac{360°}{10})$ or 36° (see Figure 2.10).

Women basket weavers among the Zulu (South Africa) and among the Subiya, Babirwa, Yei and Mbukushu in the north of Botswana (near the border with Angola) also use the coil technique. They produce basket-bowls as well as flask-shaped, pot-shaped and watertight bulb-shaped beer baskets, which are often decorated. When making the baskets in Botswana, the natural doum palm is interwoven with tannin dyed palm —the tannin dye is extracted from the roots—to produce an extraordinary variety of designs and forms. In the villages, small bowls are used for holding pounded grain; the large ones for harvesting and winnowing crops; the lidded baskets are for storage of seed and grain; the large open urn-shaped basket is for serving domestic beer. Photograph 2.2 show baskets from Botswana in the author's collection. Their designs are of the types $d4$, $d5$, $d6$ and $c3$. Figure 2.11 shows the design of type c4 of another basket bowl from Botswana.

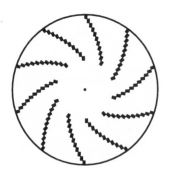

Figure 2.9

Figure 2.10

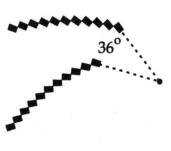

The basket weavers do not decorate their baskets at the end, but advance with their decoration of the coil, circuit by circuit. As the coil itself is not a circle or a set of concentric circles, the end product may never have exact rotational symmetry, only approximate. This leads us to pose some further questions for fieldwork among the women weavers:

- What image of the end product does the craftswoman have in her mind before she starts weaving her basket?
- How does she guarantee that her basket will display (approximately) n-fold rotational symmetry? Does she always select the number n before she starts weaving?
- How does she count, or how does she determine or measure, the distances that must exist between the successive coloured parts, when she begins to introduce the decorative motif?

As the motif begins its introduction in a certain circuit of the coil, the distance between corresponding points of successive copies of the motif should be an integral part of the length of that circuit. In other words, the distance should be equal to the length of the respective circuit divided by the intended rotational order. Figure 2.12 shows four stages of starting a decorative motif in the sixth circuit of the coil, whereby the 5-fold rotational symmetry is intended.

Figure 2.11

15

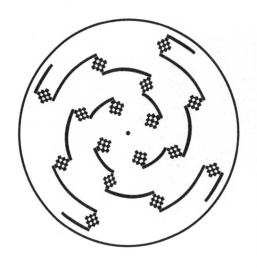

Another type of question for further fieldwork is related to the geometrical similarities between various motifs and their cultural meaning. For example, information from Botswanacraft tells us that "The motif of the triangle is the symbol of 'Swallows flying in formation'. When swallows mig-rate it is a portent of rain. It is the sign of good fortune. 'Tears of the Giraffe' are depicted by parallel lines or dots, originating from the time when women followed men on the hunt. They observed the giraffe shedding tears as the hunters closed in for the kill. To commemorate the death of the giraffe, its tears were woven into the basket. Other motifs are: the 'Forehead of the Zebra', identified by bold stripes, or a flower-like star design; the diamond shapes are, 'Knees of the Tortoise'; a zigzag line is 'Urine trail of the Bull'; curved concentric lines are 'Ribs of the Giraffe'; and the 'Running Ostrich' is a circular pattern of stepped lines" (Botswanacraft poster).

a

Figure 2.12

b

c

d

Photograph 2.1A

Photograph 21.b

Photograph 2.2C

Photograph 2.2D

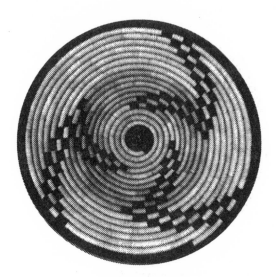

Photograph 2.3

3 MAT WEAVING

Figures 3.1 and 3.2 show mats woven from raw wool by Venda women in the far north of South Africa, near the border with Zimbabwe. Both display double (horizontal and vertical) axial symmetry.

Figure 3.3 shows another mat from the region, which displays a vertical bilateral symmetry.

Venda (South Africa)
Figure 3.1

Venda (South Africa)
Figure 3.2

Venda (South Africa)
Figure 3.3

4. BUHLOLO STRING FIGURES

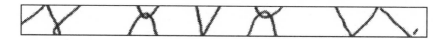

A girls' game, which was widespread among the Thonga in the Eastern Transvaal (South Africa) and the South of Mozambique, is called *ku tha buhlolo*:

"The girls take a string tied at both ends so as to form a large ring, and make all kinds of complicated figures by twisting it with their fingers and even with their lips (and teeth p.g.). Girls compete together and try to surpass each other in inventing new figures. They teach each other this *buhlolo*", writes Junod in 1912 (Vol. 1, p. 175).

Figure 4.1 shows three string figures observed by Junod. It may be noted that the first two display double symmetry (two perpendicular axes of symmetry), while the third one displays only one axis of symmetry.

QUESTIONS AND SUGGESTIONS

* Try to make yourself the string figures shown.
* How is the symmetry of the final string figures obtained? Do they correspond

to certain symmetrical movements of the fingers of both hands?

* Do girls (or boys) in your environment play with string figures? How do they learn / teach them? What do the elder women (and men) know about them? Make a collection of these string figures.
* Invent your own string figures.
* How can string figures be used in geometry teaching? Experiment!

For more information about string figures from all over the world, consult (Abraham, 1988). Haddon (1906) and Wedgwood & Schapera (1930) describe some string figures from (boys and men in) Southern Africa in general, and Botswana in particular.

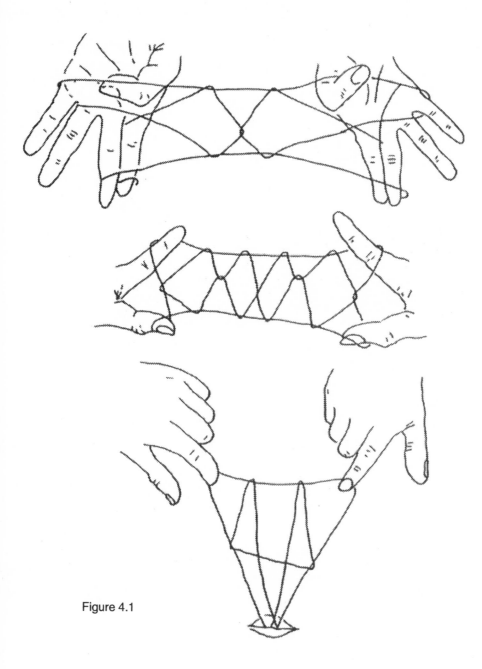

Figure 4.1

5. OKU-TALEKA
DECORATED POTTERY

Among many African peoples, pottery has been traditionally a women's craft. The pots display various shapes (see the examples in Figure 5.1) and often they are decorated with geometrical drawings. The Nyaneka-Humbe women in south-western Angola call these drawings, with which they ornament the upper part or the neck of their earthenware, *oku-taleka*. This expression derives from the verb *tala*, which means to look, or see. In other words, the drawings have to be seen, or to be looked at (Estermann, 1960, p. 197).

When the women decorate their pots, they have rotational symmetry in mind: the motif is repeated, on the neck, an entire number of times (n). If the motif itself displays an axial symmetry, then the neck design belongs to type *dn*. If not, to type *cn*, as we saw in Chapter 2. Figure 5.2 shows a decorated pot seen from below. Note the 9-fold rotational symmetry of the decoration.

Questions that can only be answered

Figure 5.1. Shapes of Southern African earthenware.

29

by fieldwork, in the case of the Nyaneka-Humbe, as well as that of other female potters in southern Africa, are

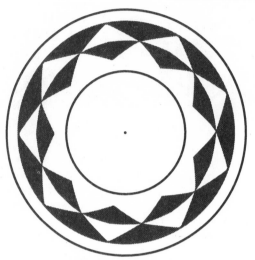

Figure 5.2.

* How do the potters guarantee that a motif can be repeated an entire number of times? Do they make measurements in one way or another? Do they estimate the size of the motif before introducing the ornamentation? Do they select the value of n before they start decorating?
* How are the replicas of the same motif produced?

Following an ornamental band around the neck of a pot, one always finds next to a certain example of the motif an exact replica of the same motif. One may continue to follow the band even after completing one circuit and, in this way, continue to find "new" copies of the motif. In this sense — as in the case of the ornamental strips on the sipatsi — one may consider an ornamental band on the neck of a pot as infinite. Consequently, one may consider the part of the band illustrated (horizontally) on a piece of paper as representing the whole band that extends infinitely to the left and to the right, always repeating the same decorative motif at a fixed distance. In other words the decorative band on the neck of a pot may be considered as a strip pattern (cf. Chapter 1 and Appendix 1).

Figure 5.3 shows some strip patterns on pots made by the Nyaneka-Humbe women. Also from Angola are the examples of strip patterns on decorated ceramics from the Lwimbi-Ngangela and the Mayaka displayed in Figures 5.4 and 5.5. Examples from Zimbabwe are presented in Figure 5.6. An example of colourful Venda ceramic decoration is shown in Figure 5.7 (extreme north of South Africa).

Figure 5.3
Oku-taleka

Figure 5.4
Lwimbi-Ngangela

Figure 5.5
Mayaka

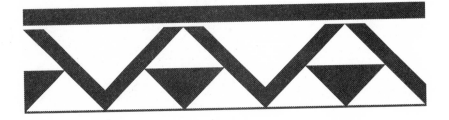

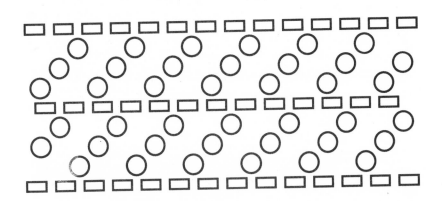

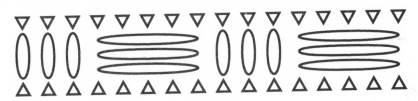

Figure 5.6
Zimbabwe

Venda
Figure 5.7

Figures 5.8 and 5.9 display examples of
strip patterns on decorated pots of the Yao
and Makonde in northern Mozambique.

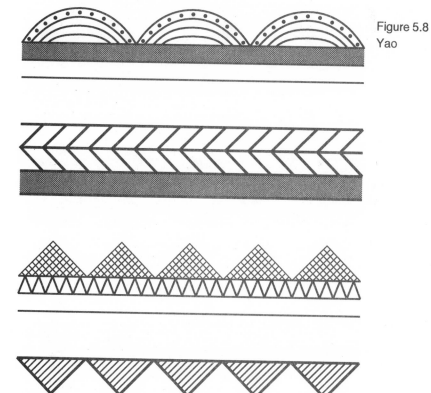

Figure 5.8
Yao

Figure 5.9
Makonde

Women's Cooperative, Maputo
Figure 5.10

Figure 5.10 shows three strip patterns on pots decorated at a women's cooperative near to Mozambique's capital, Maputo. Figure 5.11 displays a broad decorated band composed of three strip patterns on another pot from the same cooperative.

The reader is invited to analyse the symmetries of the strip patterns presented in this chapter (cf. Appendix 2).

Women's cooperative, Maputo
Figure 5.11

6. MAFIELO GRASS BROOMS

Basotho women produce a grass broom, called *lefielo* (pl. *mafielo*), with which they clean their houses, removing easily and effectively dust from difficult corners. The *lefielo* is made from *moseha* grass, which is found in the Maloti, the mountains of Lesotho (cf. Ambrose, 1976, p. 271). The grass is gathered into small bundles. The ends are turned back and bound in, making what looks like a rectangular mat. This mat is then bound tightly into a spiral with black strands of plaited horsehair. The horsehair strands themselves are often arranged to form an attractive pattern for the "handle" of the broom. Nowadays the women use green or red cotton, plastic or other artificial threads instead of horse hair. Photograph 6.1 displays some *mafielo*.

Photograph 6.1

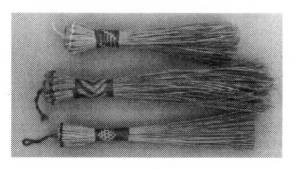

39

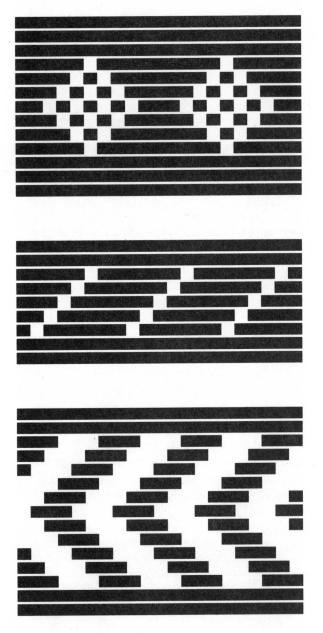

Figure 6.1

Small *mafielo*, of about 30 cm. in length, are used as decoration on house walls. The decoration of the "handles" is introduced in such a way that a given ornamental motif is repeated exactly a whole number of times.

In Figures 6.1, 6.2, 6.3, 6.4, and 6.5 we present several strip patterns visible on *mafielo* in the author's collection.

Figure 6.2

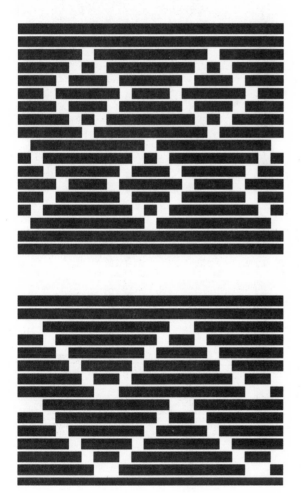

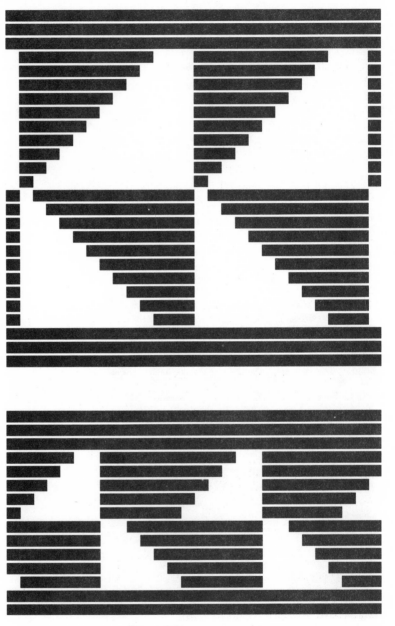

Figure 6.3

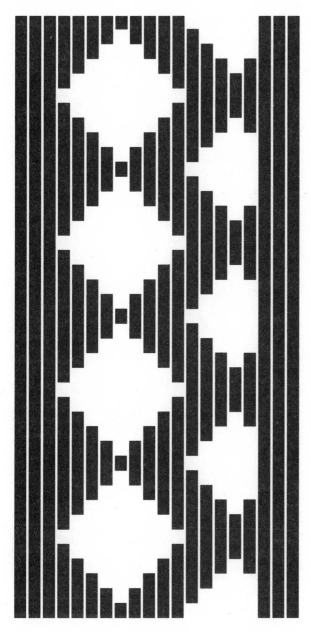

Figure 6.4

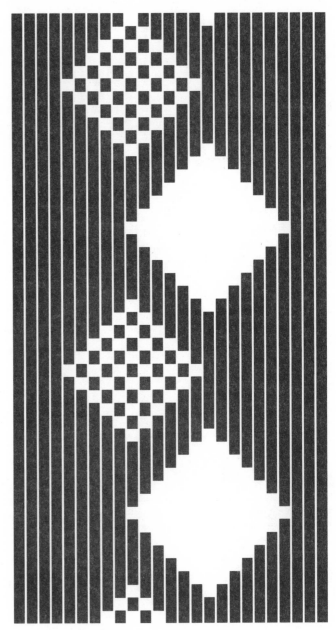

Figure 6.5

7. NEMBO—TATTOOING AND BODY PAINTING

Among most of the peoples of Mozambique tattooing of the body has been practised. For various reasons, including the negative attitude of Islam and the Christian churches towards tattooing, the tradition is vanishing. Among men, tattoos signified the change in status when passing from boyhood to adulthood, or they marked the quality of a hunter, healer or smith, etc. The role of tattoos among women was more esthetic; symbols of female beauty and of fertility (cf. Medeiros).

Tattoos may result from incisions, impregnation or, for example, from the use of caustic vegetable products. In the event of injuries, the tattooer knows how to treat them. Women were normally tattooed by other women, the Makonde in northeastern Mozambique being a notable exception (cf. Dias & Dias, p. 57).

The Yao in the northern Niassa Province call tattoos *nembo* (singular: *lulembo*). Figure 7.1, 7.2 and 7.3 present (schematically) examples of *nembo* on the breast and abdomen of Yao women. Following the basic shape of the body, these tattoos have an (vertical) axial symmetry.

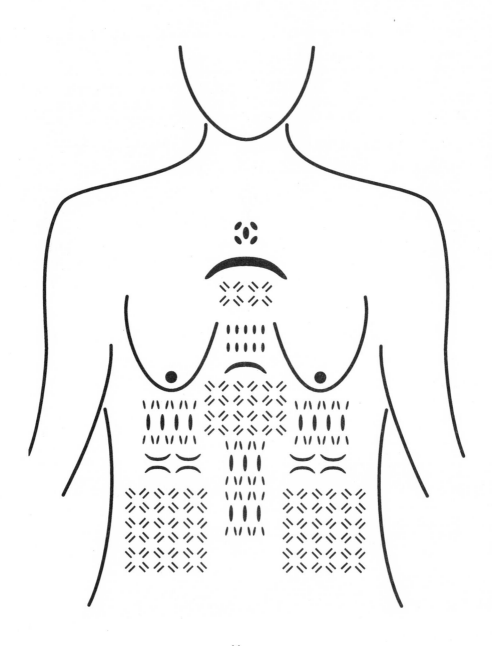

Yao
Figure 7.1

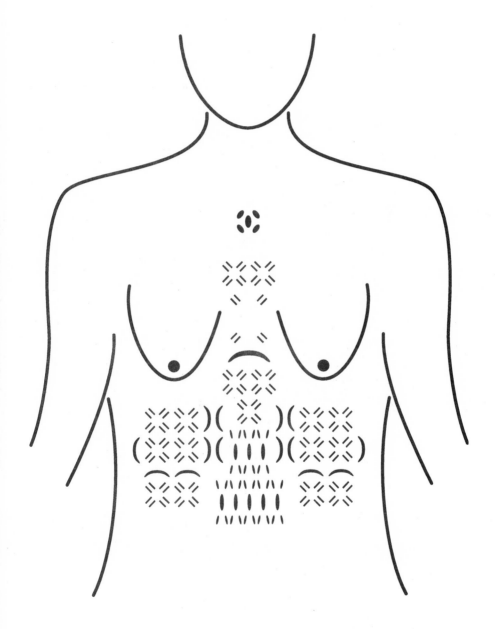

Yao
Figure 7.2

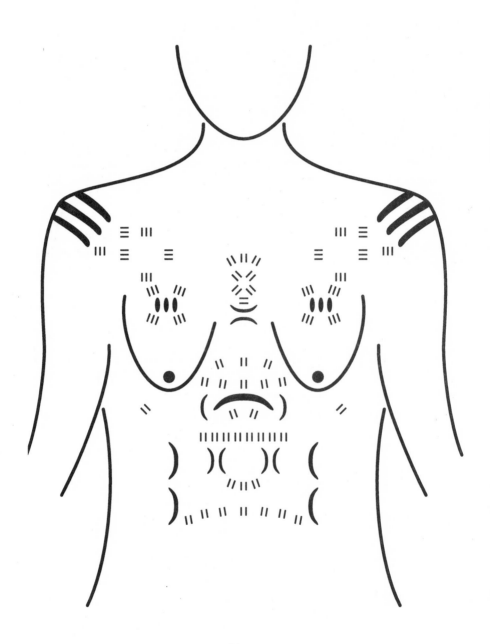

Yao

Figure 7.3

48

Details of the same *nembo* display double symmetry (two perpendicular axes of symmetry, see Figure 7.4); others have both double and fourfold rotational symmetry (see Figure 7.5).

Figure 5.4

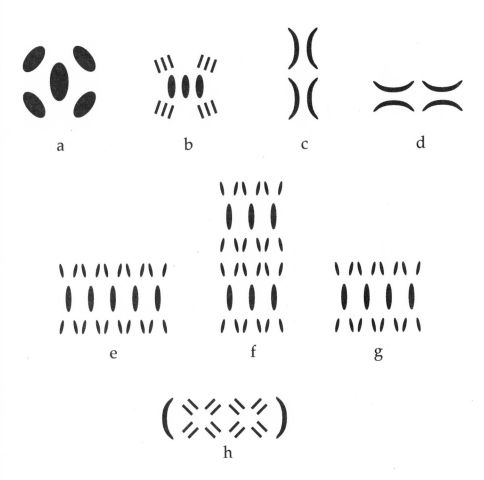

a   b   c   d

e   f   g

h

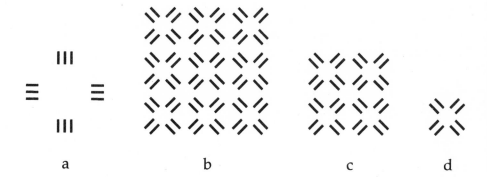

Figure 7.5

Figure 7.6 displays a tattooed Sena woman from east central Mozambique, while Figure 7.7 presents a Tsonga woman from the south of the country. Once more, the designs have bilateral symmetry and some details double symmetry (see Figure 7.8).

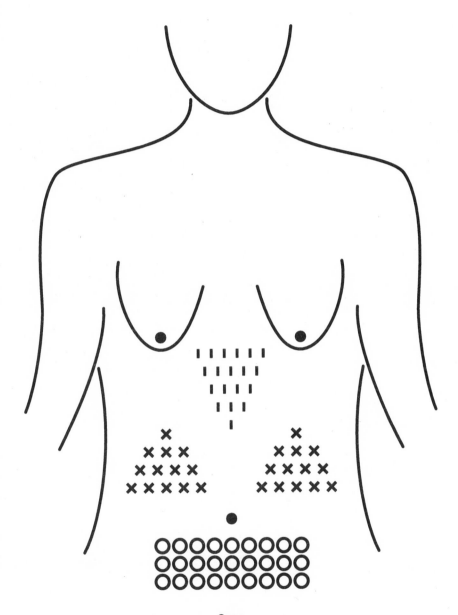

Sena
Figure 7.6

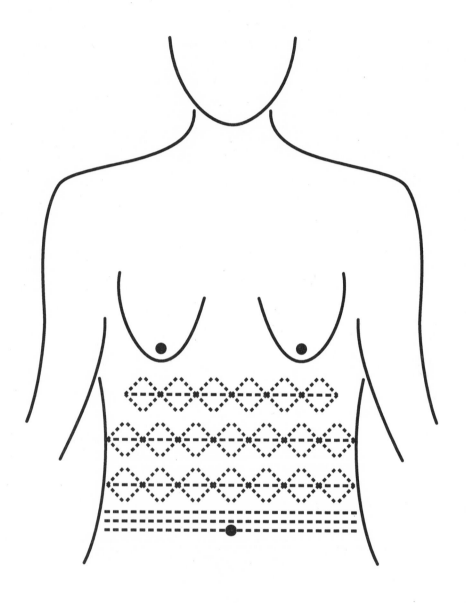

Tsonga
Figure 7.7

Figure 7.8

Figure 7.9 presents a motif tattooed on the breast of a Tsonga woman. One notes the equilateral triangles with their three-fold symmetry. On the upper back of another Tsonga woman the double symmetry design in Figure 7.10 appears.

Figure 7.9

Figure 7.10

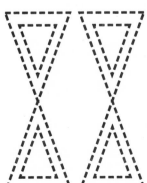

Figure 7.11

Figure 7.11 displays two tattoo motifs, with four-fold symmetry (type *d4*), used on the abdomen of Ndau women in west central Mozambique. A decorative element, with four-fold rotational symmetry of the type *c4* they use on their thigh, is presented in Figure 7.12.

Figure 7.12

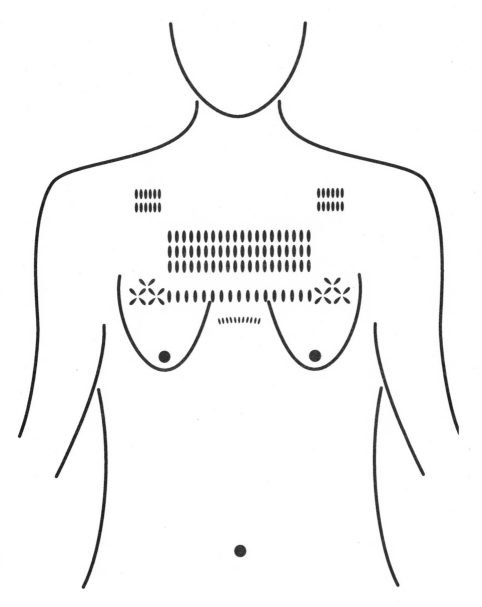

Makwa
Figure 7.13

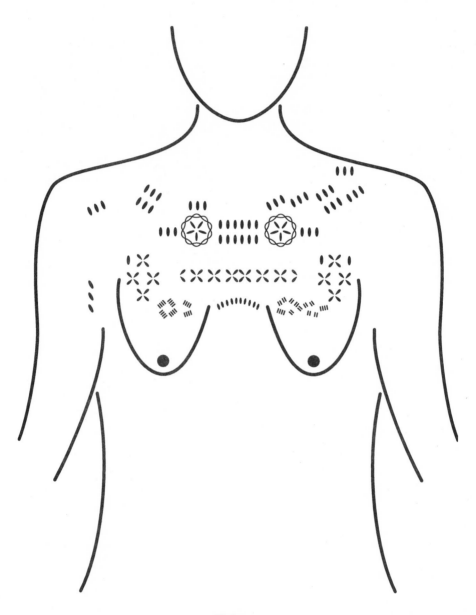

Makwa
Figure 7.14

Bilateral symmetry was also common among Makwa women in the north east of the country. Figure 7.13 gives an example. Sometimes this symmetry was consciously broken as in the example displayed in Figure 7.14. An interesting detail with five-fold symmetry is reproduced in Figure 7.15.

Figure 7.15

Examples of facial tattoos among Makwa women are shown in Figure 7.16.

Figure 7.16

Tsonga women from the southern Province of Gaza have the motif of a facial tattoo in an eight-fold rotational symmetry (see Figure 7.17).

Figure 7.17

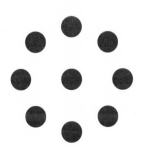

The following are some questions for fieldwork:

How is the symmetry of the final design ensured? Where does the tattooer start? At the central axis? At the left hand side? The right hand side? The top? The bottom? After concluding the first design element, where does she continue, etc. ?

Which measurements or estimations take place during this process?

Fieldwork carried out by my Yao-speaking student Salimo Saide in 1994 — studying ceramic decoration and nembo among his people — showed that it is not easy for a young school-educated man to win the necessary confidence of old female artisans and other women, either to show their tattoos or to share and explain their knowledge. Once a relationship of mutual confidence had been established, the women showed great interest in the possible ways of valuing their ancient traditions, and suggested the reproduction of their ceramic designs on capulanas (rectangular cloths worn by women around their waist and legs) and their nembo on T-shirts. Maybe new generations will learn to appreciate tattoo designs by painting them on their own and their friends bodies, or by decorating their dolls with nembo, etc. Certainly they will invent variations on old themes. This constitutes a whole field open to educational, geometric and artistic experimentation.

Among several peoples of southern Africa body painting was practised. Figure 7.18 shows a painted and masked Lwimbi-Ngangela woman from central Angola.

Lwimbi-Ngangela
Figure 7.18

8. OVILAME BEAD ORNAMENTS

Beading is traditionally a woman's craft almost all over southern Africa. Among the beautiful ornaments worn by Ovimbundu women in Angola are their *ovilame* (singular: *ulame*), a beaded diadem on the forehead. The making of the rectangular diadems demands a great deal of patience from the women. Each bead is attached twice. In the direction of the width there are, on average, between 20 and 25 beads, giving a width of between 3 and 3.8 cm. First, one threads the beads on strings in the direction of the length, between 28 and 30 cm. Then the 20 to 25 parallel strings of equal length are fastened at their ends, and thereafter with one long new string the beads are threaded once more, this time transversely, as is schematically shown in Figure 8.1. Normally red, blue, black and white are used as colours (cf. Hauenstein, 22-25). Figures 8.2 and 8.3 display strip patterns on several *ovilame*.

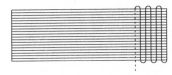

Figure 8.1

Figures 8.4 and 8.5 display examples of 19th century bead embroideries collected from southern Africa and exhibited in the Ethnological Museum in Berlin (Germany): detail of a woman's loin-cloth (Zulu, South Africa), detail of a beaded apron for young girls (Makwa, northern Mozambique), and examples of beaded embroidery on woven combs (Yao, northern Mozambique / southern Tanzania).

Further examples of beadwork from the Yao (this time also southern Malawi) in British museums are displayed in Figures 8.6, 8.7 and 8.8. They have various symmetries: bilateral symmetry (Figures 8.6 and 8.7b), double bilateral symmetry with perpendicular axes (Figures 8.5a and 8.8a), two-fold rotational symmetry (Figure 8.5b), four-fold rotational symmetry (Figure 8.7a). Figure 8.7c has a double axial two-colour symmetry: the design allows vertical and horizontal reflections which reverse the two colours, black and white. The motif repeated on a beaded girdle in Figure 8.8b admits vertical reflections which reverse black and white, and a horizontal reflection that maintains colour.

An article by Baumann (1929) shows photographs of two beaded strip patterns on headbands from the Ngangela in central Angola (see Figure 8.9).

Among the Ndebele, Xhosa and Zulu in South Africa beaded ornaments play(ed) an important role in marking changes in life.

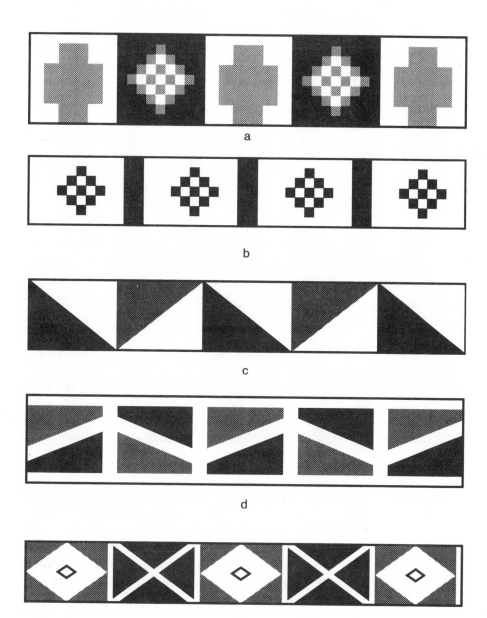

Ovilame (Ovimbundu, Angola)
Figure 8.2

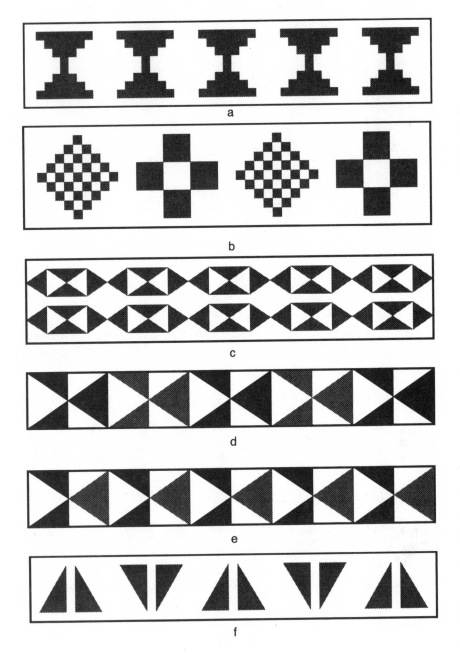

Ovilame (Ovimbundu, Angola)
Figure 8.3

A
Zulu (South Africa)

B
Makwa (Mozambique)

Figure 8.4

A

B

Yao

Figure 8.5

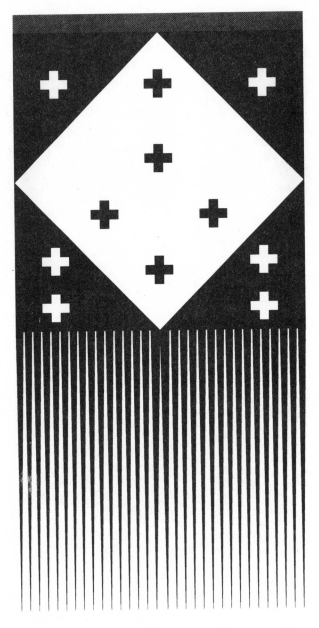

Yao
Figure 8.6

a

b

c

Yao

Figure 8.7

a

b

Yao
Figure 8.8

Yao
Figure 8.9

a

b
Ndebele (South Africa)
Figure 8.10

The beadwork worn by Ndebele women changes as a girl progresses towards her married, adult status. A small girl wears a *ghabi*, a beaded panel with a geometric motif. At puberty she will have a *pepetu*, made by her mother. At marriage there is a fresh array of beaded clothing and ornaments. The *pepetu* is substituted by the jocolo, a beaded apron about 44 cm wide by 60 cm long. A bead headdress or headband and numerous neck, arm and leg ornaments might be added. After the first few months of married life a woman is entitled to wear a new beaded apron, called *mapoto* (cf. Carey, p. 35-38). Figure 8.10a represents schematically a design on a neckpiece. The coloured motif on a beaded apron is shown in Figure 8.10b. Both designs display horizontal and vertical axes of symmetry.

Among the Xhosa, small girls wear beaded aprons and boys wear bead waist bands. When a girl likes a young man, "she will make him three headbands, all to be worn together if he accepts the first one. As the affair progresses, the girl makes arm and leg bands, numerous belts and neck ornaments ... " (Carey, p. 47).

In the early nineteenth century Zulu women made wood and shell beads, worn round the neck or waist. Later (imported) glass beads became common. Besides strings of beads worn round the neck, waist, arm or ankle, whether as one strand or doubled and twisted, rectangular panels of beadwork are produced. Long rectangular *ulimi* (tongues) are worn by men on the chest. A girl may wear a narrow strip with small rectangular panels over the chest and one

71

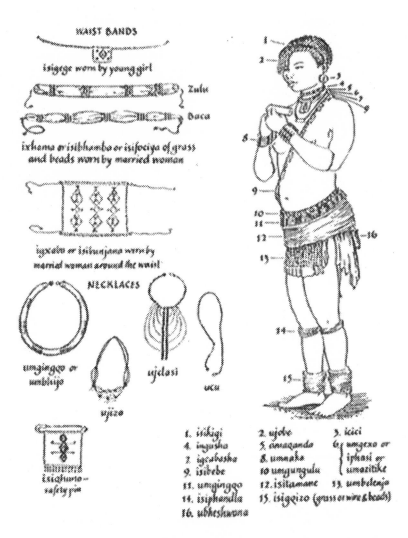

Figure 8.11

shoulder. A married woman may deck her headdress with flat strips of beadwork or with hairpins ornamented with bead panels (Cf. Grossert, p. 51-60; Carey, p. 49-59). Figure 8.11 presents an overview of bead ornaments worn by Zulu women.

Figure 8.12 shows three beaded aprons. The first two display horizontal and vertical axes of symmetry. The same double symmetry characterises the motifs in Figure 8.13 on bands of beadwork which decorate the headdress of a married woman. The individual beads of one of the principal colours are here represented by black dots. Photograph 8.1, taken in July 1994 on the beach in Durban, shows a collection of colourful beaded 'bandolets'. Figures 8.14, 8.15, 8.16, 8.17 and 8.18 display the strip pattern structure of several polychrome bandolets in the author's collection. They have different symmetries: The strip patterns in Figures 8.14a and c have vertical axes of symmetry and are invariant under a half turn about the centres of each of the zigs and zags of the central zigzagging bands. The strip pattern in Figure 8.14b is invariant under a translated reflection (see Appendix 1). The band pattern in Figure 8.15 has horizontal and vertical axes of symmetry. The reader is invited to analyse the symmetries of the strip patterns in Figures 8.16 and 8.17.

Photograph 8.1

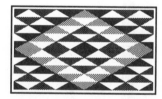

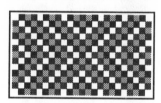

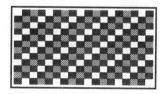

Zulu
Figure 8.12

73

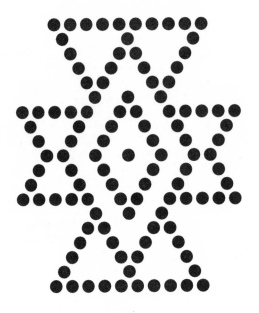

a

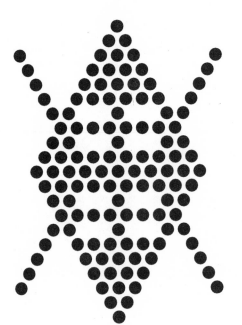

b

Figure 8.13

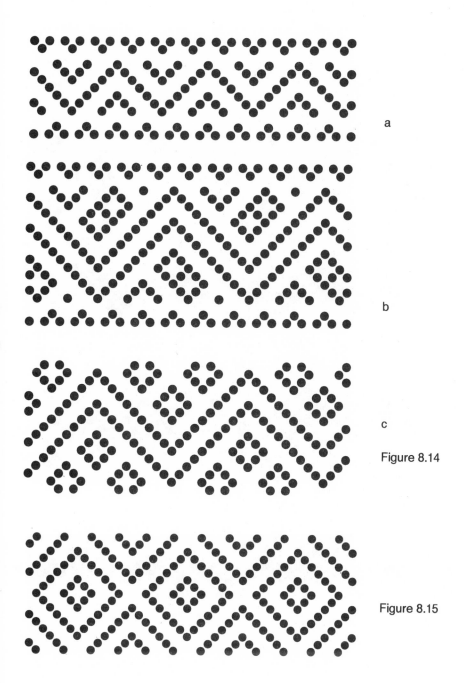

a

b

c

Figure 8.14

Figure 8.15

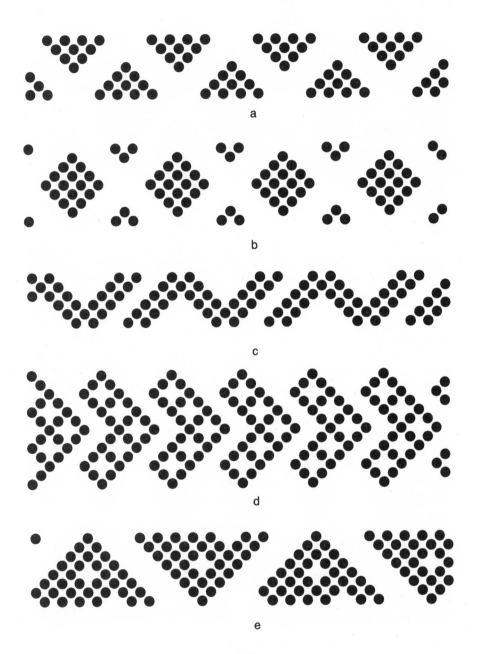

Zulu

Figure 8.16

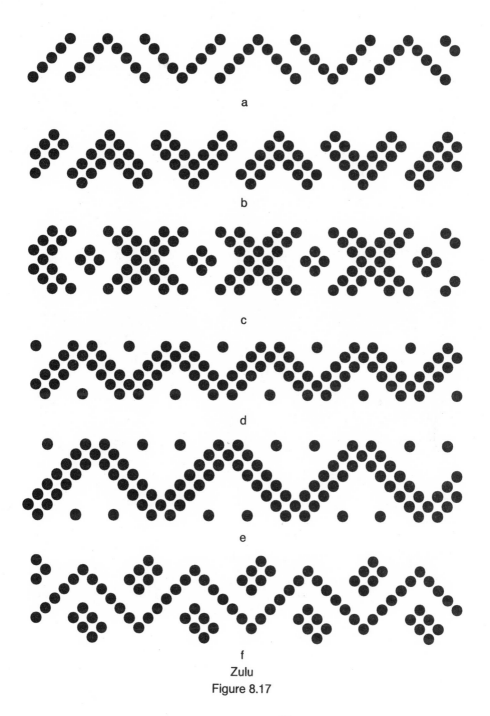

a

b

c

d

e

f

Zulu

Figure 8.17

a

b

c

d

e

f

Zulu

Figure 8.18

Figure 8.18 displays the position of beads of the two principal colours of the other Zulu bandolets in the author's collection.

The oldest surviving people of southern Africa are the San ('Bushmen'), today living in the Kalahari Desert of Botswana and Namibia. San women used to make beads out of ostrich eggshell. More recently glass beads are also used. Figures 8.19 and 8.20 display strip patterns visible on beaded headbands.

From northern Botswana are duochrome beaded aprons of which Figures 8.21 and 8.22 show details. They are made by Mbukushu women. One notes the two-colour structure of the design in Figure 8.22: It has a vertical mirror symmetry, but reflection in the horizontal axis reverses the two colours.

Figure 8.23 shows a detail of an Okavango beadwork design, once more from northern Botswana. It is really a two-dimensional pattern in the sense that it may be extended in all directions of the plane, repeating a basic cell that may be composed of two parallelograms which are symmetrical to one another: the cell allows a horizontal reflection that reverses black and white

San
Figure 8.19

San
Figure 8.20

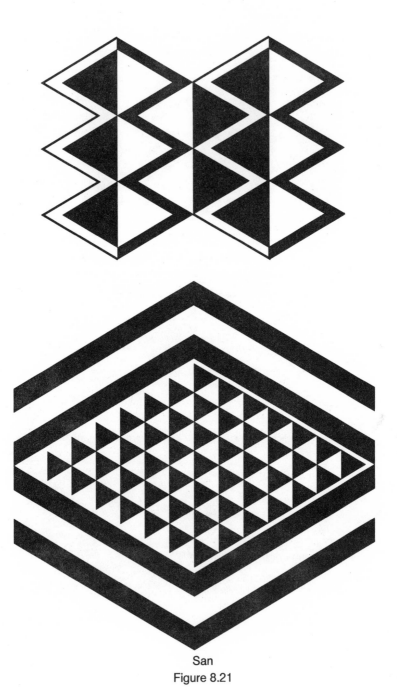

San
Figure 8.21

San
Figure 8.22

San
Figure 8.23

Figure 8.24 shows a detail of beaded 'fertility doll' from Lesotho. It is also a plane pattern. Besides white, three other colours have been used. The following cell may be repeated to produce the pattern:

Lesotho
Figure 8.24

Some questions for fieldwork, experimentation and reflection:

*   How do the women beaders learn to make their beaded bands and panels? Who teaches them?
*   How do they learn to favour symmetries? How do they themselves analyse or classify symmetries? What terminology do they use?
*   How do they produce the symmetrical

85

patterns? Which images of the final composition exist in their minds before they start to join the beads? How do these images possibly change during the production process? Which measurements or calculations are used in order to guarantee local and overall symmetrical designs?

* How is it possible to incorporate the beaders' knowledge into their further (mathematical) education?

* How is it possible to embed the beadwork tradition into (school) (mathematical) education of the children of southern Africa?

In this context, it may be worthwhile to look for more specimens of older beadwork and to compare their designs with more recent beadwork. In those regions where the beadwork tradition has been vanishing, it seems to be important to look for (the remains of) older beadwork, both in museums, private collections and, in particular, as my colleague Abdulcarimo Ismael suggested, in the containers of older women. He noted that when he was younger and still living in Mozambique's Nampula Province—inhabited principally by the Makwa—he had seen children playing with beads taken away from ornamented objects kept by their grandmothers in wooden boxes.

9. *Litema*
MURAL DECORATION

Traditionally, once the Sotho men have completed the building of their houses, their wives undertake the decoration. The walls are first neatly plastered with a mixture of mud and dung, and often coloured with natural dyes. Then they may be decorated with geometric patterns, called *litema* (sing.: *tema*). The word *litema* derives from *ho lema*, meaning to cultivate, and *tema* means a ploughed field or plot. Many *litema* designs resemble furrows made in the earth when planting.

The *litema* tradition is not of recent origin. In 1861 the missionary Casalis wrote that the Sotho houses "are in the form of a large oval oven, and are entered by creeping along a very narrow passage, which serves to prevent the wind from reaching the interior. The walls are perfectly well plastered, and often decorated with ingenious designs" (Casalis, p. 127), and, according to Gill, the *litema* patterns only appeared on the exterior of houses during the 19th century. Such patterns had previously only appeared on the interior surfaces of houses (cf. Gill, p. 29).

The most popular form of *litema*, which often appears on the cylindrical walls of the circular rondavels or on the façades of rectangular huts, consists of parallel grooves arranged in a variety of forms, sometimes suggesting floral patterns (see e.g. Figures 9.14 and 9.20). The women use forks or sticks to obtain the striped, furrowed pattern. Using the forefinger, they engrave the walls while the last coat of plastered mud is still wet. Cloths dipped in paint may be used to cover large areas of the space. Fine detail is added by using brushes. Sometimes cardboard stencils are used to repeat patterns (cf. Changuion, p. 30).

The *litema* "woman's art is seasonal. It blooms, wilts and flowers again with the passage of the seasons. It is a fugitive art. Painted on walls of mud, it dies with the temporary surface it adorns. The sun dries it and cracks it, the rain washes it away" (Changuion, p. 13). Rosie Mpofu explained to the authors of 'The African Mural' that "Before special occasions such as engagement parties, weddings, important church celebrations, Easter, or Christmas, an entire village will be redecorated. Sometimes each housewife does her own design. More often the most prestigious craftswoman of the village will be consulted. The redecorating becomes a social event. While the women drink their tea, squatting round cleared areas on the ground, the chief artist sketches various schemes in the dust. Once agreement is reached about colours and designs, the women of the village set to work while the 'artist' directs the whole procedure from a central point. If the weather is good, the work will be completed within a week" (Changuion, p. 111).

A more lasting form of *litema* decoration, employing a mosaic pattern utilizing embedded stones in mud surfaces, is frequently used in the Mafeteng area in Lesotho (see e.g. Figure 9.3).

The African Mural (Changuion, 1989) contains a beautiful collection of photographs of *litema*, mostly from Sotho houses in South Africa (Free State and Transvaal). The authors are conscious that the *litema* tradition "is in imminent danger of extinction" (Changuion, p. 11). In 1976, the National Teacher Training College (NTTC) of Lesotho published a booklet with 29 *litema* designs collected by students in order to "revive interest in worthwhile Sesotho traditions" (Mothibe, p. 2). In his presentation, the coordinator underlines that "Like other national traditions this one is in danger of dying out as more and more houses are built of concrete walls which are usually painted or white-washed. Also a growing number of women no longer like or know the art anymore" (Mothibe, p. 2).

SYMMETRY AND THE BUILDING UP OF LITEMA PATTERNS

Symmetry is one of the most basic features of the *litema* designs. One of the reasons, indicated by Changuion, for the frequent occurrence of axial or bilateral symmetry, is that "the painting functions as an extension of human action, and echoes the structure of the body. A painter, when drawing on the ground in explanation or preparation for mural painting, often draws with both hands. She begins at the top of an imaginary vertical, and the resultant forms on either side of this are simultaneously realized and are mirror-images of each other" (Changuion, p. 35, 36).

Most *litema* designs — and all the *litema* reproduced in this book — are built up from basic squares, which constitute as it were the (unit) cells of the design. The women lay out a network of squares, and then they reproduce the basic pattern in each of them. The number of reproductions or repetitions of the unit cells depends, in practice, on the available space on the wall or floor to be decorated.

As a convention, we will represent all the *litema* in this book in the same manner: four rows each containing four times the unit cell. When we look at the 16-basic-squares representation, we can imagine the pattern extending indefinitely or infinitely, that is as far as we like, to left, to the right, upwards, downwards, or in all other directions in the same plane as the drawing.

The symmetries of a whole *tema* design depend on the symmetries of the unit cell, and the on the way in which the design is built up from its basic squares, as we will see now. Which methods do Sotho women use for the building up or construction of their *litema*?

ONE-SQUARE-PATTERNS

The following square constitutes the unit cell of the *tema* called Lithebe (see

Figure 9.1)

One sees that this cell is repeated, in exactly the same position, in all the horizontal rows and all the vertical columns of the Lithebe pattern. This is a rather exceptional situation. Figures 9.2, 9.3 and 9.4 present three more examples. We may call this type of designs a one-square-pattern.

TWO-SQUARE-PATTERNS

In most *litema*, the unit cell appears in various positions.

Let us consider the *tema* called Maqoapi (see Figure 9.5). Here the basic cell appears in two distinct positions, the normal initial one:

and reflected about its vertical axis:

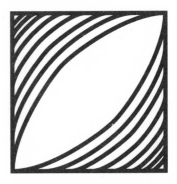

The Maqoapi pattern is composed of double columns in which a rectangle constituted of two unit cells, one in the normal and the other in the vertically reflected position are repeated. We may call a pattern built up like the *tema* Maqoapi a two-square-pattern.

FOUR-SQUARE-PATTERNS

In many *litema*, however, the unit cell appears in four different positions and the whole design is built up out of repetitions of 2x2 squares composed of four times the unit cell in each of the four positions. One example constitutes the *tema* called Bochabe (see Figure 9.6; note that the unit squares themselves are not made visible). Here the unit cell is the following:

(1)

Immediately below the unit cell in this position (1), another one appears in a horizontally reflected position (2):

(2)

Immediately to the right of the first unit cell (1), another one is drawn (3), this time reflected about a vertical axis:

(3)

The fourth unit square (4), that is the cell immediately to the right of the second cell and below the third one, is vertically reflected in relation to the second and, in addition, horizontally reflected in relation to the third:

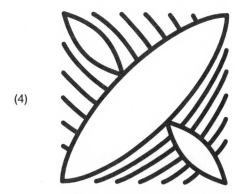

(4)

In other words, the fourth position is derived from the initial position by a rotation of the cell through a straight angle (an angle of 180°). As already mentioned, the whole design is now composed of double rows with 2x2 squares with the unit square in its four positions:

1	3
2	4

These larger, new 2x2 cells display double (axial) symmetry. They are invariant under reflections about the central vertical and horizontal axes. We may call this type of design a four-square-pattern.

95

In this example of the Bochabe pattern there are additional diagonal axes of symmetry, as a consequence of the axial symmetry of the initial unit cell:

In the same manner as the Bochabe pattern, the *litema* Lesira (Figure 9.7) and Baemane (Figure 9.8) are also built up. In the last case, the four distinct positions of the unit cell reduce to only two, as (1) = (4) and (2) = (3), as a consequence of the invariance of the initial unit cell under a rotation through a straight angle:

In other words, if, in the plane of the drawing, one rotates this unit cell through a straight angle about the centre of the square, we obtain exactly the same figure.

If one uses the unit cell of the Maqoapi design (Figure 9.5) and builds up a four-square-pattern instead of the Maqoapi two-square-pattern, one obtains a pattern (see Figure 9.9), with which a Tswana woman decorated her courtyard wall (Botswana). In this case the basic cell is not only invariant under a half turn, but displays two diagonal axes of symmetry:

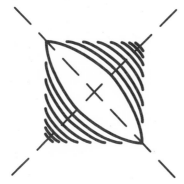

One can observe that the same 2x2 square may also be obtained by rotating the unit cell three times through a right angle about the right bottom vertex of the initial cell and copying it each time after rotating.

If one builds up a one-square-pattern using the same unit cell, one obtains Figure 9.10, very similar to the *tema* in Figure 9.3 that is made out of black and white stones and where the squares themselves became invisible.

The situation whereby the unit cell has two diagonal axes of symmetry also occurs, for instance, in the four-square-patterns Likilisa (Figure 9.11), Boriba (Figure 9.12), Mohloa (Figure 9.13), Sekho (Figure 9.14), Mofapo (Figure 9.17), Melebo (Figure 9.18) and Figure 9.15 (cf. Figure 9.9). *Litema* built up as four-square-patterns, but with a unit cell that displays only one diagonal axis of symmetry, are, for example, Bochabe (Figure 9.6), Lesira (Figure 9.7), Mefapo (Figure 9.16), Mokolobe (Figure 9.19), Likhole (Figure 9.20), Ketane (Figure 9.21), Maoka (Figure 9.22), Malente (Figure 9.23), Litepo (Figure 9.24), and Maletere (Figure 9.25). The only example of a four-square-pattern with a unit cell that does not display any symmetry is the *tema* Mahloa (Figure 9.26).

One may build up new four-square-patterns by using the unit cells of one- or two-square-patterns. For example, Figure 9.27 shows the pattern one obtains in the case of Lithebe unit cell (Figure 9.1). Experiment yourself!

QUESTIONS AND SUGGESTIONS

* Invent new unit cells and build up your own one- two- or four-square-patterns in the way Sotho women build up their *litema*.

* Experiment with the unit cells of the *litema* presented in this chapter, and try to build up new patterns that are not one-, two- or four-square-patterns in the way described. We present some examples in Figures 9.28 (its unit cell comes from Figure 9.5), 9.29, 9.30, 9.31, 9.32 (their unit cell comes from Figure 9.11), 9.33, 9.34, and 9.35 (their unit cell comes from Figure 9.7).

A SPECIAL TYPE OF FOUR-SQUARE-PATTERNS

Several painted *litema*, and others whereby changes in the relief of the dung surface of the plaster suggest two distinct colours, may be represented on paper as black-and-white patterns.

The 'black-and-white' *litema* in Figures 9.36 and 9.37 are four-square-patterns built up in the same way as were described in the preceding section.

The *tema* in Figure 9.38 is, however, built up in a slightly different way. Its basic square is the following:

(1)

Immediately below the basic square there is another square

(2)

which may be obtained by reflecting the unit cell horizontally, but ... by interchanging its colours at the same time: what was black before now becomes white and what was white before, now becomes black. In other words, this new square is the 'negative' (in photographic terms) of the horizontally reflected unit cell:

unit cell

horizontally reflected
('positive')

horizontally reflected
('negative')

Something similar happened to the square immediately to the right of the unit cell:

(3)

This results from vertically reflecting the unit cell and thereafter interchanging black and white:

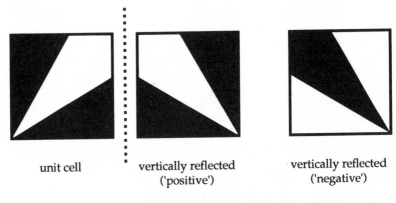

| unit cell | vertically reflected ('positive') | vertically reflected ('negative') |

The fourth square may be obtained by reflecting the second vertically and then taking the negative, or by reflecting the third horizontally and then taking the negative, or by rotating the initial unit cell through a straight angle, with the same result:

(4)

The basis of the four-square-pattern now displays two axes of reflection which reverse (or interchange) the colours:

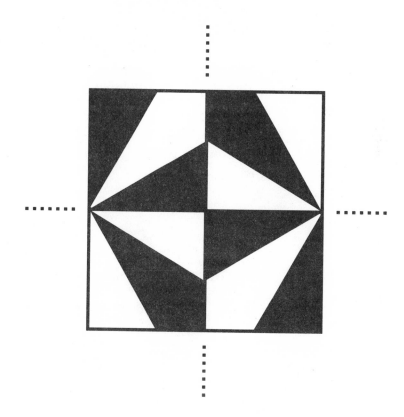

Figures 9.39 to 9.49 show a series of *litema* which are built up in the same way. The initial unit cells have their own peculiarities.

In the aforementioned example the unit cell displays an axial symmetry:

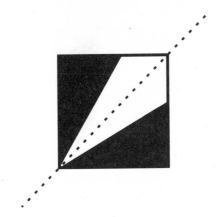

It is a normal reflection, that is, the colours are preserved. In consequence, the entire (infinite) pattern allows horizontal and vertical reflections which reverse black and white, and diagonal reflections which maintain the colours:

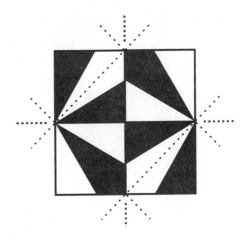

The unit cell of the pattern in Figure 9.39 allows two diagonal reflections which maintain colour:

The unit cell of the pattern in Figure 9.40 allows horizontal and vertical reflections which maintain colour, and diagonal reflections which reverse colour:

The unit cell of the pattern in Figure 9.41 allows a half turn around its centre which reverses colour:

The unit cell of the pattern in Figure 9.42 allows one diagonal reflection which reverses colour:

The unit cell of the pattern in Figure 9.43 allows one diagonal reflection which maintains colour, and another diagonal reflection which reverses colour. In addition a half turn around the centre reverses black and white:

The *litema* in Figures 9.44, 9.45, and 9.46 are characterised by the same symmetries.

In the case of the unit cell of the *litema* in Figures 9.47 and 9.48, the two diagonals change roles:

This time, reflection about the diagonal that goes up from left to right maintains colour, whereas reflection about the diagonal that goes down from left to right reverses black and white.

The attractive *tema* in Figure 9.49 is very unusual. Its inventor constructed unit cells that allow reflections about both their diagonals, which interchange black and white:

The unit cells of the *litema* in Figures 9.50 and 9.51 display horizontal and vertical axes of symmetry. This time, white lines separate the differently coloured regions of the pattern:

QUESTIONS AND SUGGESTIONS

* Compare Figure 9.52 with the *tema* in Figure 9.37. Where do the differences in building up these patterns lie?

* Compare Figure 9.53 with the *tema* in Figure 9.47. Where do the differences in building up these patterns lie?

* Observe Figures 9.54, 9.55 and 9.56. In which way are they differently built up from the unit cell of the *tema* reproduced in Figure 9.46?

Take the unit cells of some other *litema*, and build up new patterns in the same way used in constructing Figures 9.54, 9.55 and 9.56.

* Compare Figures 9.57 and 9.58 with the *tema* in Figure 9.39. Where do the differences in building up these patterns lie? Are these new patterns also four-square-patterns or not? How may one characterise them?

*   Compare Figure 9.59 with the *tema* in Figure 9.43. Where does the difference in their respective building up lie? Try to construct new patterns by changing the unit cells of other black-and-white *litema* in a similar way.

*   Consider Sotho black-and-white four-square-patterns with horizontal and vertical reflections which interchange colour. We have seen that their unit cells often display symmetries: reflections in their horizontal, vertical and diagonal axes which may or may not reverse the colours. Try to find all possibilities for combination of these reflections, and for each possibility invent patterns that correspond to the respective possibility, that is, belong to the respective class.

    For example, the *litema* in Figures 9.43, 9.44, 9.45 and 9.46 belong to the same class, as they allow a reflection which maintains colour about the diagonal that go does down from left to right, and, simultaneously, a reflection about the other diagonal which reverses colour.

*   If rotational symmetry of 90 and 180 degrees is also permitted, what new possibilities emerge?

*   In the painting of the attractive *tema* in Figure 9.60, white lines separate some of the coloured regions. Four different colours are used. Try to con-

struct new patterns introducing white lines and four colours in a similar way to the black-and-white *litema* reproduced in this chapter.

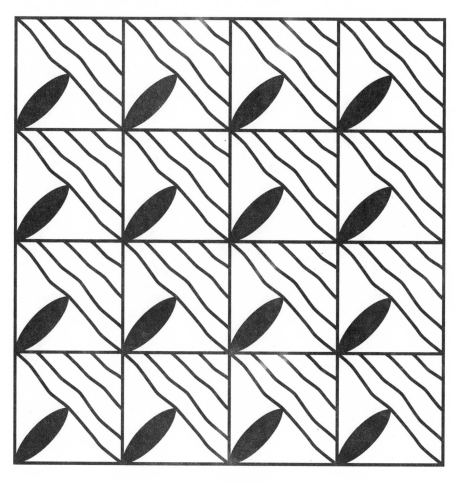

tema Lithebe
Figure 9.1

Lesotho
Figure 9.2

Lesotho
Figure 9.3

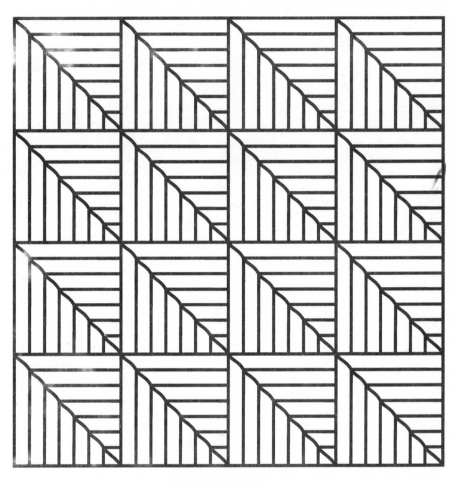

tema Moraba-raba
Figure 9.4

tema Maqoapi
Figure 9.5

tema Bochabe
Figure 9.6

tema Lesira
Figure 9.7

117

tema Baemane
Figure 9.8

Botswana
Figure 9.9

Figure 9.10

tema Likilisa
Figure 9.11

tema Boriba
Figure 9.12

tema Mohloa
Figure 9.13

tema Sekho
Figure 9.14

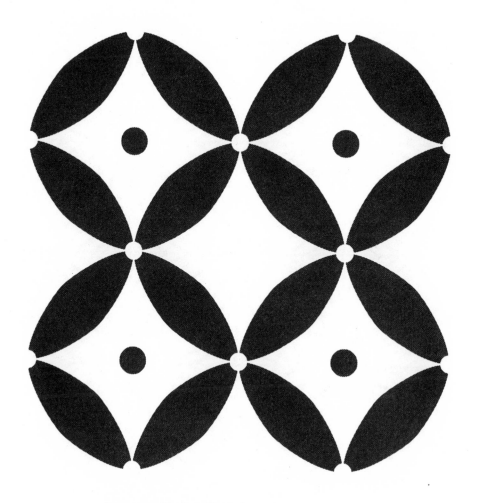

tema near Qacha's Neck (Lesotho)
Figure 9.15

tema Mefapo
Figure 9.16

tema Mofapo
Figure 9.17

tema Melebo
Figure 9.18

tema Mokolobe
Figure 9.19

tema Likhole
Figure 9.20

tema Ketane
Figure 9.21

tema Maoka
Figure 9.22

tema Malente
Figure 9.23

tema Litepo
Figure 9.24

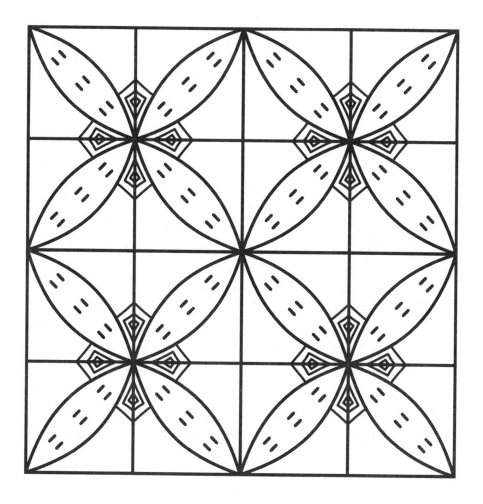

tema Maletere
Figure 9.25

tema Mahloa
Figure 9.26

variant
Figure 9.27

variant
Figure 9.28

variant
Figure 9.29

variant
Figure 9.30

variant
Figure 9.31

variant
Figure 9.32

variant
Figure 9.33

variant
Figure 9.34

variant
Figure 9.35

Sotho (Northern Free State, South Africa)
Figure 9.36

Sotho (Southern Transvaal, South Africa)
Figure 9.37

Sotho (Southern Free State)
Figure 9.38

Sotho (Easthern Free State)
Figure 9.39

Sotho (Transvaal, Orange Free State border)
Figure 9.40

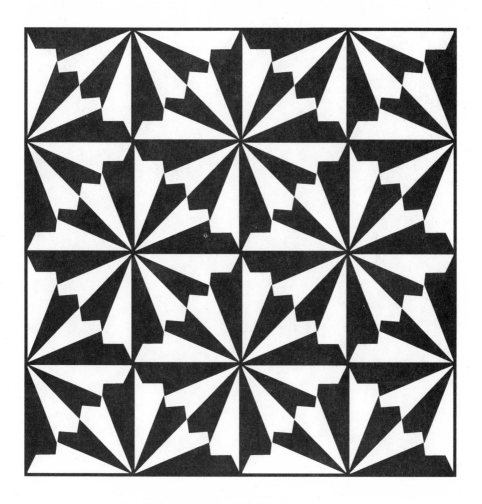

Sotho (Southern Free State)
Figure 9.41

Sotho (Eastern Free State)
Figure 9.42

Sotho (Eastern Free State)
Figure 9.43

Sotho (Eastern Free State)
Figure 9.44

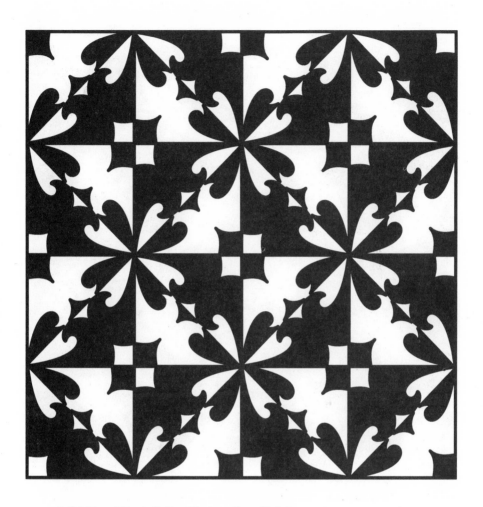

Artist Mavel Dani, Sotho (Eastern Free State)
Figure 9.45

tema in Teyateyaneng (Lesotho)
Figure 9.46

Artist Mavel Dani, Sotho (Eastern Free State)
Figure 9.47

Lesotho
Figure 9.48

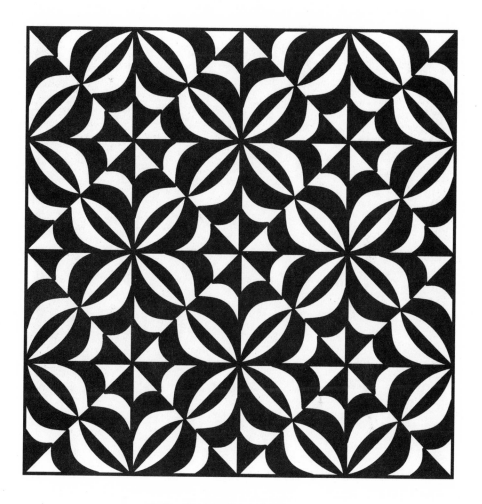

Sotho (Eastern Free State)
Figure 9.49

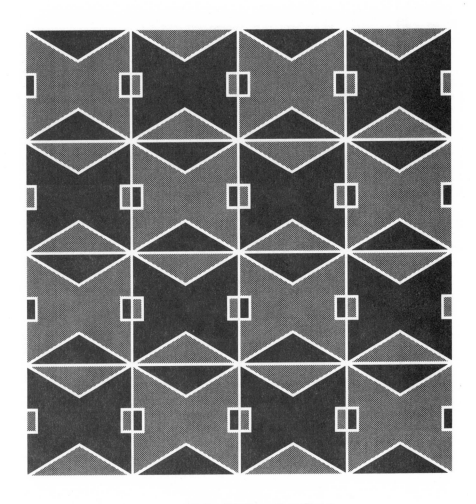

Sotho (Northern Free State)
Figure 9.50

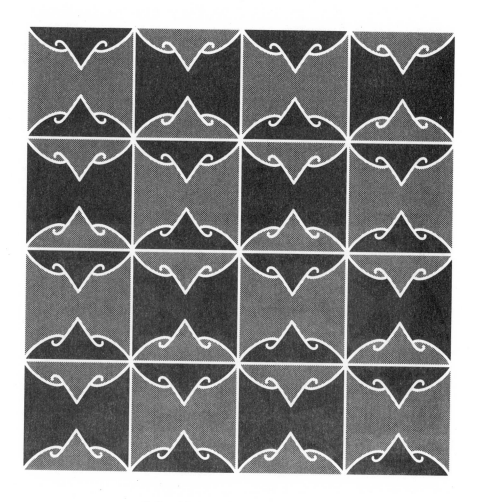

Sotho (Northern Free State)
Figure 9.51

variant

Figure 9.52

variant
Figure 9.53

variant
Figure 9.54

variant
Figure 9.55

variant
Figure 9.56

variant
Figure 9.57

variant
Figure 9.58

variant
Figure 9.59

Sotho (Northern Free State
Figure 9.60

10. IKGHUPTA— MURAL DECORATION

Mural decoration is not unique to the Sotho. The Ndebele women, living north of Johannesburg in South Africa's Transvaal Province, also decorate the walls of their houses. Their traditional style of geometric patterns scratched with the fingers into the cow dung and mud wall surface, is called *ikghuptu*. What sets them apart from the Sotho *litema* are the characteristics of the geometric designs and the addition of painted lines. The paints were originally white, red, and yellow, natural soot, ash and clay ochres obtained from the earth. The beginning of the 20th century saw the introduction of a new colour, blue, coming from commercial washing blue. Powder paints followed and, in more recent years, acrylic paints with their bright colours, highly appreciated by the Ndebele have been used (see photograph 10.1). The new style of decoration using commercial paints is called *pewulani* (cf. Courtney-Clarke).

Just as ceremonial beadwork marks female maturational stages and marital status (see Chapter 8), so does Ndebele house decoration accompany the passage from girlhood to womanhood. It is at puberty,

Photograph 10.1

during the winter months of July and August following the young men's initiation, that the young women are confined to the home and are taught among other "secrets of womanhood" the art, geometry and techniques of beadwork and mural decoration.

Ndebele mural decoration involves both the exterior and interior walls of the traditional family homestead, called *umuzi*. The umuzi consists of a main house—called an *indlu*—, circular or rectangular, several (semi)detached separate dwellings for boys and girls, and the cooking hut. Around the complex is a low wall, which has either an elaborate entrance or a simple gatepost. Other low walls divide the area within the homestead, creating courtyards. The walls are woven from twigs and sticks between wooden poles first fixed into the ground. The women then plaster the framework of the walls on both sides with a mixture of clay and cow dung. This procedure may take several months to complete. When the dwelling is dried, painting begins (cf. Courtney-Clarke, p. 28).

Decorations vary from year to year. After the summer rains have washed away the paint work, the women of the village resurface the walls with cow dung and mud and redecorate.

The Ndebele women begin their murals with freehand painting of white-wash outlines to form the basic motifs, which are then filled in with elaborate (colourful) designs.

Elliot (1989) and, in particular, Courtney-Clarke (1986) have published beautiful collections of photographs of Ndebele murals.

Figure 10.1 presents a detail of a front wall. The design has a (global) bilateral symmetry, and is composed of rectangular motifs. Figure 10.2 displays the back wall of another house. The design as a whole, as well as its constituent elements (see Figure 10.3), display double (axial) symmetry.

Figure 10.1

Figure 10.2

a   b

Figure 10.3

Figure 10.4, with the same double symmetry, shows part of one of the house walls of an *umuzi*. The murals of the entire homestead were redecorated for the occasion of a family wedding, using, in the case of the displayed wall, only black soil from a nearby river.

Figure 10.4

The designs with which two gateposts of a house in the Middelburg district are decorated, are presented in Figure 10.5.

a

b

Figure 10.5

Figure 10.6 shows a black-and-white motif on a low wall.

Figure 10.7 displays a mural on a house wall in Pieterskraal in former KwaNdebele. One notes the door and windows. Below, on the right hand side appears a decorated rectangle with two-fold rotational symmetry, that is, the design is invariant under a half turn (see Figure 10.8).

Figure 10.6

Figure 10.7

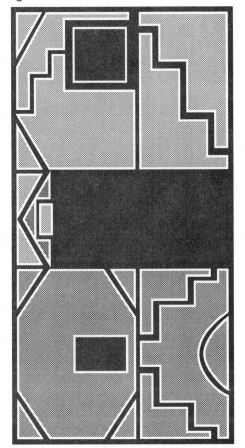

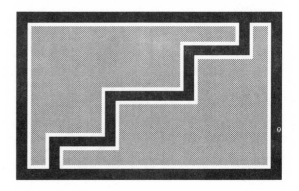

Figure 10.8

The wall detail shown in Figure 10.9 is from the same village. This time the axial symmetry is broken by half turn symmetry in the middle (see Figure 10.10).

Two-dimensional plane patterns, of the type seen in Chapter 9 when analysing *litema* mural decoration, are not constructed by the Ndebele women. However, one-dimensional strip patterns do appear, as the examples in Figure 10.11 illustrate.

The repeating motif in Figure 10.11e is very special (see Figure 10.12a). It seems to derive from the two-colour pattern in Figure 10.12b. A vertical reflection reverses black and white. In the Ndebele motif the white areas (Figure 10.12b) have been replaced by black-and-white strokes.

Figure 10.9

Figure 10.10

Several authors refer to the art and craft of the Ndebele women as an "endangered art-form" (Levinsohn, p. 129), as a consequence of the "encroachment of western civilization" (Elliot, 1989, p. 11): "Many young people leave their traditional homesteads to attend schools, and then move on to the cities to work" (Elliot), and decorating the houses has "become either too expensive or there is a declining concern among the younger generation not interested in preserving their culture" (Levinsohn). The resettlement policy of apartheid has had a destructive influence on the cultural development of the Ndebele population (cf. Courtney-Clarke). In post-apartheid South Africa, it may be possible to revalue the rich tradition of the Ndebele craftswomen artistically, geometrically and educationally.

Figure 10.11

a

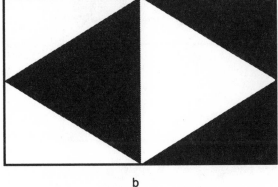

b

Figure 10.12

In other parts of southern Africa — outside the sphere of the Ndebele *ikghuptu* and Sotho *litema* — it may be possible to find and develop mural decoration traditions in numerous ways. Figure 10.13 shows the painted front wall of a house in Swaziland.

181

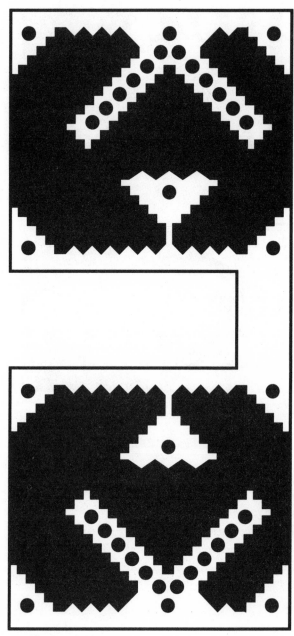

Figure 10.13

11. Pythagoras a Woman?

Example of an Educational-Mathematical Examination

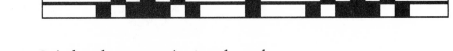

Ovimbundu women in Angola make baskets using the coil technique (see Chapter 2 on coiled basketry). They decorate their baskets with ornaments which are introduced step by step going upwards along the circuits of the coil. Figure 11.1 shows a detail of eight successive circuits where a snake is represented through the contrast between black and white.

Representation of a snake
Figure 11.1

The Ovimbundu designs in Figures
11.2, 11.3, 11.4, 11.5, 11.6 and 11.7 are symmetrical.

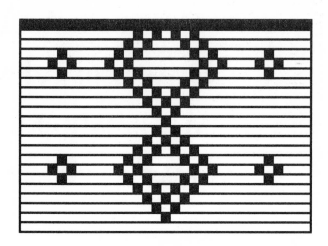

Hoe
Figure 11.2

Omakuva, birds' feet
Figure 11.3

Ovisanja, leaves of a dried tree
Figure 11.4

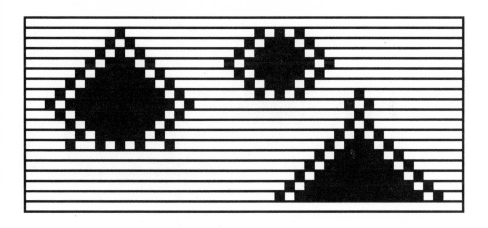

Akimba
Figure 11.5

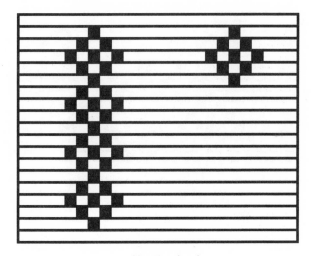

Alende, clouds
Figure 11.6

a

b
Alesu, kerchief or scarf
Figure 11.7

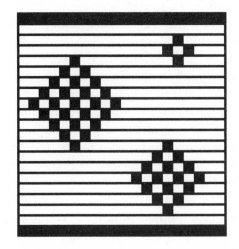

Ovipapa
Figure 11.8

In Figures 11.2, 11.3, 11.7b and 11.8 we
see the same type of design we have already

seen in earlier chapters (Figures 2.8, 2.11, 6.2a, 6.6, 8.2a, 8.2b, 8.3b, 8.5a, 8.9a,): a type of a black-and-white "toothed square" with 2 (examples in Figures 11.2 and 11.7b), 3 (e.g. Figure 11.6), 4 (e.g. Figure 11.7.b and 11.8), and 5 (e.g. Figure 11.7b) black teeth on each side. In my book *African Pythagoras. A Study in Culture and Mathematics Education,* I showed how these "toothed squares" may be examined in an educational context to (re)discover or (re)invent the Pythagoras' Theorem and to find an (infinite) series of proofs for this proposition (cf. also Gerdes, 1988). Here I will reproduce only the basic heuristic idea.

Looking at the number of unit squares on each row of the "toothed square" in Figure 11.9, it is easy to see that the area of a "toothed square" is equal to the sum of areas of the 4x4 shaded square and 3x3 unshaded square.

A "toothed square", especially one with many teeth, looks almost like a real square. So naturally the following question arises: is it possible to transform a toothed square into a real square of the same area? By experimentation, the pupils may be led to draw the conclusion that this is indeed possible (see Figure 11.10).

In Figure 11.9, we have seen that the area of a toothed square (T) is equal to the sum of the areas of two smaller squares (A and B):

$$T = A + B.$$

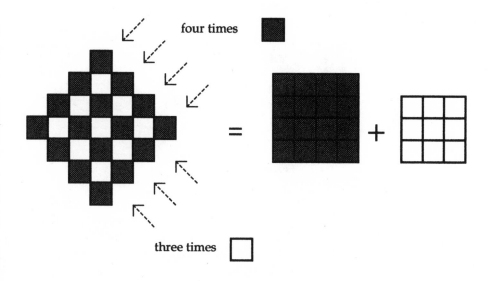

four times

three times

Figure 11.9

From Figure 11.10 we concluded that the area of a toothed square (T) is equal to the area of a 'real' square (C). Since C = T, we may conclude that
A + B = C.

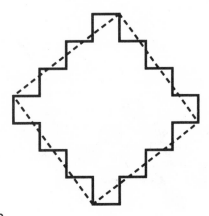

Figure 11.10

Do other relationships between these three squares exist? What happens if one draws the toothed square and the two real squares (into which it is decomposed) together (e.g. on square grid paper), in such a way that they become 'neighbours'? When we now draw the last real square (area C) on the same figure, we arrive at the Pythagorean Theorem for the case of (a,b,c) right-angled triangles with $a:b = n:(n+1)$, where the initial "toothed square" has $n+1$ teeth on each side. Figure 11.11 illustrates the Pythagorean Proposition for the special case of the (3,4,5) right-angled triangle. On the basis of these and further experiments (see Gerdes, 1988, 1992, 1994), the pupils may be led to conjecture the Pythagorean Theorem in general.

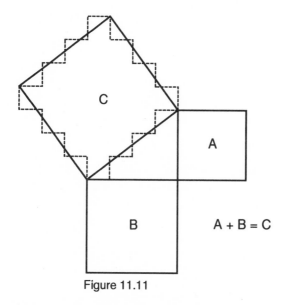

Figure 11.11

The "toothed squares" and "toothed triangles" may also be examined educationally in other ways, as the following examples will show.

EXAMPLE 1

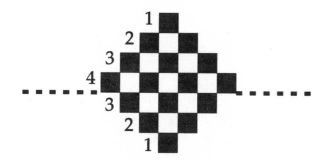

Figure 11.12

Let us consider a "toothed square" and count the number of black unit squares in each of the horizontal rows (see Figure 11.12). We already know that the total number of black unit squares is a square number, in this case 4^2. Comparing the two enumerations, one finds:

$1 + 2 + 3 + 4 + 3 + 2 + 1 = 4^2$,

or, taking into consideration the dotted divisionary line:

$(1 + 2 + 3 + 4) + (3 + 2 + 1) = 4^2$.

It follows that

$(1 + 2 + 3) + (3 + 2 + 1) = 4^2 - 4$,

and

$1 + 2 + 3 = \dfrac{4^2 - 4}{2}$.

Experimentation with other "toothed squares", varying the number of teeth on the side, may lead to the extrapolation

$1 + 2 + 3 + \ldots + (n-1) = \dfrac{n^2 - n}{2}$,

where n denotes a natural number bigger than 1.

EXAMPLE 2

Let us observe the upper part of Figure 11.12 and count both the black and the white unit squares row by row. For the black unit squares, one finds $1 + 2 + 3 + 4$. For the white ones (see the right side of Figure 11.13), one finds $1 + 2 + 3$. The total sum of unit squares of the "toothed triangle" is thus equal to

$$(1+2+3+4) + (1+2+3),$$
or $(1+2+3+4) + (3+2+1)$,

which was the sum of all black unit squares of the original "toothed square", that is 4^2.

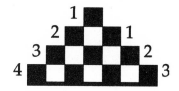

Figure 11.13

By counting all the unit squares of the "toothed triangle", row by row, irrespective of their colour, one finds $1+3+5+7$. Comparing the two enumerations one may conclude

$$1+3+5+7 = 4^2.$$

In other words, the sum of the first four odd numbers is 4^2. Experimentation with other "toothed triangles" and comparison of the results may lead to the discovery of the general result that the sum of the first n odd numbers is equal to n^2.

EXAMPLE 3

Let us now return to the expression
$(1+2+3+4) + (3+2+1) = 4^2$.
It may be transformed into
$(1+2+3) + (1+2+3+4) = 4^2$.

Similar expressions may be obtained by varying the number of teeth on the side of the "toothed square":

$$1 \qquad\qquad\qquad = 1^2 ,$$
$$1 + \qquad (1+2) \quad = 2^2 ,$$

$$(1+2) + (1+2+3) = 3^2,$$
$$(1+2+3) + (1+2+3+4) = 4^2,$$
$$(1+2+3+4) + (1+2+3+4+5) = 5^2, \text{ etc.}$$

Summing the left sides and summing the right sides, the resulting sums must be equal. Therefore, one finds:

$$2 \times [1 + (1+2) + (1+2+3) + (1+2+3+4)] + (1+2+3+4+5) = 1^2 + 2^2 + 3^2 + 4^2 + 5^2,$$

or

$$1 + (1+2) + (1+2+3) + (1+2+3+4)$$
$$= \frac{(1^2 + 2^2 + 3^2 + 4^2 + 5^2 - (1+2+3+4+5))}{2}$$

In the same way

$$1 + (1+2) + (1+2+3) + (1+2+3+4) + (1+2+3+4+5) =$$
$$\frac{1^2 + 2^2 + 3^2 + 4^2 + 5^2 + 6^2(1+2+3+4+5+6)}{2},$$

etc.

Let us look more carefully at the left handsides of the first equation and write the different expressions to be added underneath each other, like

$$1$$
$$1+2$$
$$1+2+3$$
$$1+2+3+4.$$

Their sum may be calculated vertically, that is by counting the number of 1's, 2's, 3's and 4's. One finds

$$4 \times 1 + 3 \times 2 + 2 \times 3 + 1 \times 4.$$

In the case of the second equation, one finds

$$5x1 + 4x2 + 3x3 + 2x4 + 1x5.$$

Both expressions are symmetrical. Extrapolation for an arbitrary n, leads to another symmetrical expression

$$nx1 + (n-1)x2 + (n-2)x3 + ... + 3x(n-2) + 2x(n-1) + 1xn.$$

Extrapolation on the right handside of the equations in question leads to:

$$\frac{1^2 + 2^2 + 3^2 + ... + (n+1)^2 - (1+2+3+...+[n+1])}{2}$$

As both sides have to be equal, one discovers the following equation:

$$nx1 + (n-1)x2 + (n-2)x3 + ... + 3x(n-2) + 2x(n-1) + 1xn =$$
$$\frac{1^2 + 2^2 + 3^2 + ... + (n+1)^2 - (1+2+3+...+[n+1])}{2}.$$

Test this conjecture for several values of n. How can you prove the general conjecture?

Try to find other conjectures by examining decorative ornaments, in particular those produced by women in Southern Africa.

EPILOGUE

In this book more attention has been paid to certain countries and peoples (or linguistic groups) in southern Africa than to others. This does not imply any value judgement; it is completely accidental, reflecting the limited data available to the author. The book does not pretend to be complete or exhaustive. It intends to attract attention to the geometric art(isanship) of women in southern Africa in general. It intends to stimulate further research; it intends to arouse interest in the mathematical-cultural, artistic-technological, and educational valuing of the female traditions under consideration.

Interdisciplinary research is vital: artisans, artists, geometers, cultural anthropologists, historians, ethnomathematicians, educationalists ... have to work closely together. All possible sources have to be examined, ranging from existing written sources, photographs, drawings, through private and museum collections, to fieldwork. Fieldwork may contribute to answers to such questions as

- How do/did the girls acquire the values, the techniques, and the knowledge from their mothers? How do/did the craftswomen develop their geometrical ideas, creativity and imagination? How did they develop their traditions under changing historical conditions, possibilities, and pressures? In which other spheres of life may their artistic-scientific potential be used, applied, continued, realized?
- How may the women's educational tradition become central

to, become the backbone of, any further 'adult education' 'programme': what do they want to learn and to explore? In what ways may their heritage be incorporated, be embedded, into the (curricular and extra-curricular) education of their daughters (and sons), and of all other daughters and sons all over southern Africa?

In any reflection on mathematics education in southern Africa the following profound studies should be taken into account.

- *The challenge to the South*, The Report of the South Commission, led by the former President of Tanzania, Julius Nyerere, criticizes development strategies that minimize cultural factors. Such strategies only provoke indifference, alienation and social discord. The development strategies followed up to now "have often failed to utilize the enormous reserves of traditional wisdom and of creativity and enterprise in the countries of the Third World". Instead, the cultural wellsprings of the South should feed the process of development (Nyerere, p.46).

- UNESCO's study *African Thoughts on the Prospects of Education for All* sees African cultural identity as the springboard of their development effort (UNESCO, p.10). Africa needs *culture-oriented education*, that would ensure the survival of African cultures, if it emphasized originality of thought and encouraged the virtue of creativity (UNESCO, p.15). Scientific appreciation of African cultural elements and experience is considered to be "one sure way of getting Africans to see science as a means of understanding their cultures and as a tool to serve and advance their cultures" (UNESCO, p.23).

- *Educate or Perish: Africa's Impass and Prospects*, a study directed by the historian Ki-Zerbo, shows that today's African educational system favours foreign consumption without generating a culture that is both compatible with the original civilization and truly promising. Unadapted and elitist, the existing educational system feeds the crisis by producing economically and socially unadapted people, and by being heedless of entire sections of the active population. Education for all, as discussed by Ki-Zerbo, should be an attempt to encourage the development of initiative, curiosity, critical awareness,

198

individual responsibility, respect for collective rules, and a taste for manual work. Africa needs a "new educational system, properly rooted in both society and environment, and therefore apt to generate the *self-confidence from which imagination springs*" (Ki-Zerbo, p.104). Reminding us of the African proverb "*When lost, it's better to return to a familiar point before rushing on*", Ki-Zerbo underlines that "Africa is in serious trouble, not because its people have no foundations to stand on, but because ever since the colonial period, they have had their foundations removed from under them" (Ki-Zerbo, p.82). This is certainly true in the case of mathematics.

Here lies one of the principal challenges to mathematics educators in Africa in general, and in southern Africa in particular. Many boys and girls in school experience mathematics as a rather strange and useless subject which, if not wholly imported from outside Africa, is at best 'assembled' in Africa like bicycles and cars. Here lies a challenge: the African cultural heritage should be the starting point in the development of the mathematics curriculum in order to improve its quality, to augment the *cultural* and *social self-confidence* of *all* pupils, both girls and boys.

Ethnomathematical research may contribute to finding some answers. Ethnomathematical studies analyse
* mathematical traditions which have survived colonization and mathematical activities in people's daily lives, and ways to incorporate them into the curriculum;
* cultural elements which may serve as a starting point for doing and elaborating mathematics in and outside school.

One objective of ethnomathematical research consists of looking for possibilities of improving the teaching of mathematics by embedding it into the cultural context of pupils and teachers. A type of mathematics education is intended which succeeds in valuing the scientific knowledge inherent in the culture by using this knowledge to lay the foundations for providing quicker and better access to the scientific heritage of the whole of humanity. The female heritage of southern Africa constitutes, in my opinion, a fundamental starting point for the improvement of the quality of mathematics education. It is hoped that the suggestions presented in this book may stimulate new research initiatives and educational experiments.

To those readers who are interested in knowing more about culture and mathematics education, and about ethnomathematical research, the author recommends *Mathematical enculturation* (Bishop), *Mathematics Education and Culture* (ed. Bishop), *Sociocultural bases of mathematics education* (D'Ambrosio), *Etnomatemática* (D'Ambrosio), *Ethnomathematics: a multicultural view of mathematical ideas* (Ascher), *Etnomatemática: Cultura, Matemática, Educação* (Gerdes), *Ethnomathematics and education in Africa* (Gerdes), and Zaslavsky's classic *Africa Counts: Number and Pattern in African Culture*. Doumbia and Pil present interesting examples of the use of west African games in mathematics education. For more information about current research in ethnomathematics in general, consult the Newsletter of the International Studygroup on Ethnomathematics, [1] and on research in ethnomathematics and the history of mathematics in Africa, consult the AMUCHMA-Newsletter. [2] For information about mathematics education in Africa, consult the AMUCME-Newsletter.[3]

Symmetry is central to the geometry of the female artists and artisans of southern Africa. To those readers who like to broaden their geometrical knowledge of symmetry, the author recommends *Symmetries of Culture* (Washburn & Crowe) and *Tilings and Patterns* (Grünbaum & Shephard). Weyl's classical *Symmetry* may serve as an introduction to a group theoretic viewpoint. About the (reasons for the) emergence of symmetry in nature, consult, for instance, *Fearful Symmetry − Is God a Geometer?* (Stewart & Golubitsky). Migdoll's *Field guide to the butterflies of southern Africa* presents colourful examples of bilateral symmetry. Interesting overviews of the appearance and use of symmetry and culture, are inserted in the books edited by Hargittai, *Symmetry: Unifying Human Understanding*, *Spiral Symmetry*, and *Fivefold Symmetry*, that includes also by the author on fivefold symmetry and (basket) weaving in various cultures. *Symmetry: Culture and Science*, a quarterly edited by the International Society for the Interdisciplinary Study of Symmetry, is a unique journal on the scientific study of symmetry in cultures all over the world.[4]

Maputo, March 27, 1995

NOTES

1. Editor ISGEm Newsletter P.Scott, Department of
    Curriculum and Instruction, New Mexico State University,
    P.O. Box 30001, MSC3CUR, Las Cruces, NM 88003, USA.
    ISGEm coordinator for southern Africa is D. Mtetwa,
    Faculty of Education, University of Zimbabwe, Mount
    Pleasant, Harare, Zimbabwe. Distributor of the ISGEm
    Newsletter in South Africa is Mathume Bopape, Box 131,
    Sesesho, 0742 Pietersburg.
2. Editors P.Gerdes (Mozambique) and A.Djebbar (Algeria).
    AMUCHMA stands for African Mathematical Union —
    Commission on the History of Mathematics in Africa.
3. Editor C. Julie (South Africa), c/o Department of
    Didactics, University of the Western Cape, Private Bag
    X17, Bellville 7530. AMUCME stands for African
    Mathematical Union—Commission on Methematics
    Education.
4. Editors G.Darvas and D.Nagy, ISIS-Symmetry, P.O.Box 4,
    Budapest, H-1361 Hungary

Appendix 1
On the Geometry of Pottery Decoration by Yao Women (Nyassa Province)

Presentation of the author
Salimo Saide

I was born June 20, 1965 in Lichinga, capital of the Nyassa Province. There I went to primary and secondary school. From 1985 to 1987 I took part in a teacher education program and from 1987 to 1991 I taught Mathematics and Physics at the secondary school of Pemba, capital of the Cabo Delgado Province. In that province I coordinated the local Mathematics Olympiads. In 1991 I came to the nation's capital Maputo, in the south, to continue my studies and in 1996 concluded my 'Licenciatura' in Mathematics and Physics Teaching at the 'Universidade Pedagógica'.

In 1977 I had the opportunity to read a book written by the priest Yohana, entitled "Wa'yaowe", which means "We the Yao people". It opened a whole new horizon for me. I was lucky to be able to read and write Yao since in school only Portuguese is taught. During my youth I loved to read more in Yao, but there did not exist any opportunities. By the time I went to Maputo to continue my studies, I thought my dream had died. However, when I first took part in a voluntary "circle of interest" on mathematical elements in African cultures and then in the optional course "Ethnomathematics and Education" my dream started to live again. I found a strong link between mathematics and the art of my grandparents. My participation in the course brought back memories of my land, let me remember my grandmother, her decorated mats and baskets, and her beautiful *nembo* – tattoos (see Chapter 7) and pot decorations. An idea "caught" me, I decided to research this art, and within the context of the Ethnomathematics Research Project I had the opportunity to do fieldwork in Nyassa in the periods June-July 1994, January 1995 and January-February 1996. As the theme of my research I chose the geometry of ceramic pot ornamentation. Now, after having finished my university program, I hope to return to my land, to continue my research and to teach mathematics integrating the *nembo* of the Yao people.

In my report I will deal with the following: pottery among the Yao, extracts of interviews with craftswomen, the tools used and the principal decorative motifs.

POTTERY AMONG THE YAO

Among the Yao, pottery has traditionally been a women's craft and art. The ornamentation of earthenware with geometrical patterns is dying out, I had to find and interview older craftswomen. Once found, I needed to win their confidence before they would explain their knowledge to me; this was generally not easy for me as a young man. Sometimes they were only willing to talk with me about their profession on the second or third day, after I had presented them with little gifts such as soap or 'capulanas' (woven cloths women like to wrap around their waist). My suggestions that their patterns might be used in the future to decorate 'capulanas' and scarves, and so doing will contribute to the preservation and valuing of the fruits of their creative imagination, pleased all of them.

The word *nembo* which will frequently be used in this text, means tattoo, and also designates any cicatrice voluntarily made by somebody. It is in this sense that the decorative bands on ceramic pots are known as nembo sya iwiga, that is, tattoos of the pots.

EXTRACTS OF INTERVIEWS WITH CRAFTSWOMEN

Kalua Laisi, about 70 years old, lives 40 km east of Lichinga (the Nyassa provincial capital) in a village called Ciwaya. She learnt the craft when she was twelve years old. Her neighbours made pots and, hidden away in the field, she tried to imitate them.

Initially she produced undecorated pots, which were distributed among her family. When she started to produce pots to be sold, she felt obliged to decorate them both through the influence of her girlfriends and the demand of the market. The first motifs she used were *nembo sya mikomelo* and *nembo sya maweswe*. The patterns she chose were inspired by fragments of pots she had found in abandoned places. She never worked in a group and never taught the craft to somebody else.

Jenethy Kaisi, about 70 years old, lives 30 km east of Lichinga in a village called Mbalalu. She learnt the craft from her grandmothers when she young. First she learnt to produce pots, and later she started to decorate them with ornamental strips. The first motifs she learnt, were *nembo sya mikomelo* and *nembo sya maweswe*, "because these are easy to learn", she said. She knows two other types of decorative motifs: *nembo sya maweswe ge usyausye* and *nembo sya maweswe ga suyungusya*.

Alaika Ali (or Akachocho, her artists name), about 60 years old, lives in the outskirts of Lucimwa-Ngongoti, a village in the Unango District, about 20 km of the district's capital. She learnt to make pots at a very young age, because her family was too poor to be able to buy pots. It was sufficient to observe some master craftswomen in order to try the first steps by herself. She does not remember the decorative motifs she learnt, but she recalls that in the time of her grandmothers there were more and more differ-

entiated patterns because of the competi-
tion in the market. The big demand also
stimulated the execution of the various
steps with more precision and care than in
more recent years.

Alaita Aidi, about 80 years old, lives
in the Unango District, in the village of
Ngongoti. She learnt the craft of pottery
before she took part, of the age of 8, in her
initiation rites. She learnt the craft from her
grandmother, to whom she was very close
and who was a great potter. She learnt the
decorative art from her sister-in-law, who
was a better decorator than her grandmother. Initially she executed only the easier
motifs, like *lusondo* and *masweswe*.
According to her, the decorative art
demands a great deal of imagination. The
lines are not drawn in an arbitrary way.
There are rules and sequences to be respect-
ed, and as a result, it is possible to identify
a pot's maker from the pot and its motif.
Today all this has died out, because of the
war and 'modern times' (*cisungo*).

Abaina Bulaimo, about 75 years old,
lives in the outskirts of Maniamba, capital of
the district with the same name. She learnt
the craft from her mother when she was
about ten years old. Initially she learnt to
make small pots *(iwiga yamwana)* and some
decorative motifs. Long ago she knew many
decorative motifs. Today she does not
remember most of them, using only the
lusondo motif, with which it is easy to
impress. Her grandmothers also practiced
decorative motifs. With the wars and the

arrival of white men and modern pots, the traditional craft started to wane.

Ambiti Chimbongue, about 85 years of age, presented the majority of decorative motifs by drawing them on the ground, since she (already for a considerable time) does not decorate pots any more. She lives in the Madimba district, in one of the suburbs of the districts' capital. She learned to make pots from her mother when she was still very young. In her turn her mother had learned from Ambiti's grandmother who died before she was born. Ambiti's mother told her that the grandmother had been a great master of decoration, and that, when they lived in Sanga, a lot of people from outside came to buy her pots. Ambiti Chimbongue was born in Sanga, her father was a hunter and therefore the family traveled a lot. She explains that most of the figures she illustrates "died long ago", before they had great social value, such as beautiful body tattoos. *Nembo sya maguluka* is the motif she likes most. She was very surprised in my interest in her drawings and after various encounters we had during a period of two weeks, she invited me to come and talk with her again, if she would be still alive...

TOOLS

The principal tools used for the execution of decorative bands are:

* A sharp piece of bamboo, called *lusonga lwa nnasi* (see Figure A.1);

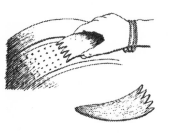

Figure A.1

* A toothed piece made of a gourd, called *cipandingwa can'gao* (see Figure A.2);

Figure A.2

* A piece made of iron or of a gourd called *nguambo*.

In order to trace parallel lines, both oblique, vertical or horizontal, the potters use the bamboo piece. To impress figures they use the *nguambo* or the *cipandingwa*. What distinguishes the artists is their knowledge of how to use the tools and combine the decorative motifs in such a way that they produce ornaments that please the eye.

The choice of decorative motifs depends largely on the type of pot to be ornamented. The principal pot types are: *lulo* or *luulo*, *didjandje* or *mauni*, *ciulogo*, *mtala* and *mkala*. Due to their shape pots of the *ciulogo* and *mtala* types are more frequently decorated.

PRINCIPAL DECORATIVE PATTERNS

1 Masweswe

The most frequently used decorative motif is *nembo sya masweswe*. It is made by first tracing two horizontal parallel straight lines with a distance of three or four fingers apart (about 5 cm). These lines are called *lusiki—lukokosi* and are traced with the *lusonga lwa nnasi* tool with two teeth.

Equidistant points are then impressed on the whole bottom line, using the *cipandingwa can'gao*. The decorators estimate with care the fixed distance between two consecutive points in order to guarantee that the distance between the last and the first point is also equal to this constant.

Starting from two neigbouring points on this line two oblique lines are drawn (called *magwandulule* or *mbundila*) that intersect on the top line. In this way a first (isosceles) triangle appears. This triangle constitutes the decorative motif. Afterwards a whole row of triangles congruent with the first one are constructed (see Figure A.3).

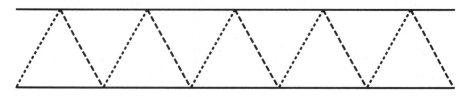

Figure A.3

Having concluded the triangles, one traces with the piece of bamboo, an equal number of oblique lines within each triangle. In Figure A.4 two possible phases for doing so are shown.

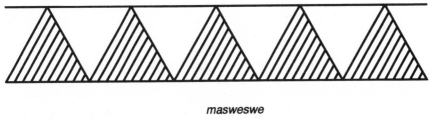

masweswe

a

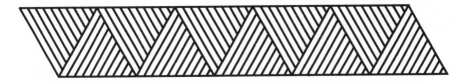

masweswe ge usyausye

b

Figure A.4

Jenethy Kaisi uses also the parabolic variant *masweswe gasyungusya* (see the lower band in Figure A.5).

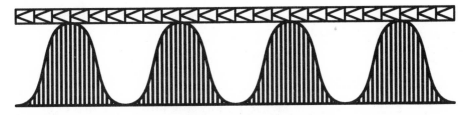

masweswe gasyungusya

Figure A.5

For Alaika Ali there exists only one type of *nembo sya masweswe* that may be used in combination with other decorative bands as the example in Figure A.6 illustrates, where the *masweswe* motif appears in the upper band.

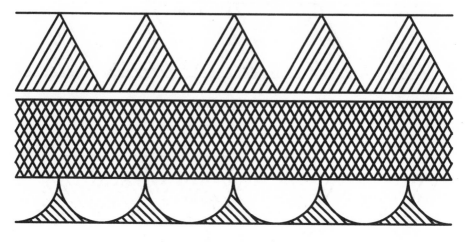

masweswe in combination with other motifs
Figure A.6

2. *Nembo sya isakulo*

The decorative motif *nembo sya isakulo* has the form of the teeth of a comb or the backbone of a fish (see Figure A.7).

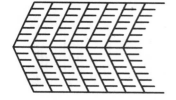

nembo sya isakulo
Figure A.7

According to Kalua Laisi, this decorative motif is essentially drawn first tracing a horizontal *lusiki* line on the upper part of the pot and then another, parallel to the first one on a lower part of the pot. Within the band formed by these two horizontal lines parallel oblique lines, *magwandulule*, are drawn completing the whole band around the pot. To guarantee that the separation of the lines is always the same—*gangatadikan-ganya*—, one uses the piece of gourd with two teeth. Next one cleans with a smooth stone those line parts that are outside the band. Once this last operation is completed, one again takes the piece of bamboo *lusonga lwa nnasi* and marks horizontal segments, that touch the oblique lines. These are short parallel lines, and their total number on each oblique line is five or six.

According Alaika Ali, this *isakulo* motif may be executed in another order. One starts by tracing equidistant parallel oblique lines with a sharp piece of bamboo. She explains that this was formerly done with an appropriate measuring instrument. For her, however, it is sufficient to pay attention. Next one marks on each oblique line a series of horizontal line segments. The number and size of these segments is constant. Finally, one traces at the top and at the bottom two horizontal lines, called *npumbulu*. *Npumbulu* literally means the cord that women fasten around their hips during certain rituals. The decoration may be completed with other ceremonial bands, for example, with *matipfa, sondo* and *mikomelo* strips as in Figure A.8. The *isakulo* motif appears more frequently in the Lichinga District than in the other districts that I visited.

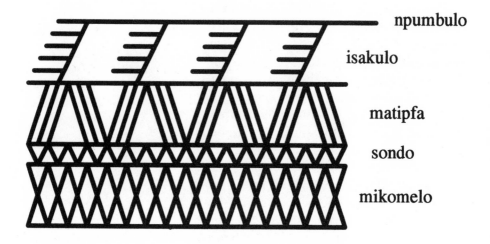

npumbulo

isakulo

matipfa

sondo

mikomelo

isakulo motif in combination
with other decorative strip patterns
Figure A.8

3. *Nembo sya lusondo*

The *nembo sya lusondo* motif is impressed with a spatula of gourd that ends in the form of a V. According to Kaluwa Laisi, this decorative motif is the easiest of all. One creates a series of triangles between two parallel lines, by placing the vertex of the V either at the bottom (V) or at the top (L) during the impression (the result is the same – see the third band in Figure A.8). In this way the *nembo sya lusondo* decorative motif is produced.

When one joins two bands, the lower with the vertices at the bottom and the upper one with the vertices at the top, and then fills up the rhombi with line segments, one obtains Figure A.9.

214

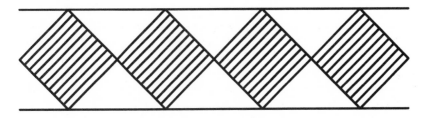

Figure A.9

Abaina Bulaimo, who learned pottery making before the "war of the Germans" (First World War) says that a long time ago she was accustomed to drawing many decorative motifs, *nasimanyidilaga mitundu djedjinji*, but today she does not remember the majority of them. She can only draw a *nemba sya lusondo*, because that is still easy at her age. Figure A.10 shows it in combination with other motifs.

masondo

Figure A.10

These days she still impresses the variant *masondo gan'pingo*, which literally means, "impressed in groups" (see the example in Figure A.11).

215

masondo gan'pingo
Figure A.11

Other impressions are also made in groups by adapting the form of the spatula of gourd. For example, Figure A.12 shows the impression of a group of small circles. This motif is more popular on pots of the *mtala* type.

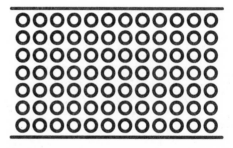

Figure A.12

4. *Nembo sya nkomelo*

Nkomelo is a wooden cube specially created to prepare the bark of trees for weaving, after the bark has been cured in water for a long time. On one of the faces of the cube (see Figure A.13) lines are drawn with some inclination (the angle is normal-

216

ly less than 45°) using a knife or some other cutting device. Over these lines another set of lines congruent to the first ones, and making the supplementary angle with the side of the square face, are drawn. The final image is that of rhombi.

nkomelo tool
Figure A.13

The *nembo sya nkomelo* motif (see Figure A.14) is inspired by this instrument. The only difference lies in the way it is constructed. This time one uses a spatula of bamboo and the concurrent lines are known as *magwandulule, makalasulo* or *ndambala*.

nembo sya nkomelo
Figure A.14

Alaita Aidi describes the construction as follows: "I first trace one oblique line inclined to the right. From this first line *ndambala*, I mark the distance, where at the end I will trace the second line parallel to the first *(syegonele imóimó)*, and so successively until completing the whole. On the top of these I trace the second group of

217

ndambala but this time with the lines inclined to the left. The distance between them is the same as before. In this way we obtain the *nembo sya nkomelo* motif".

5. *Nembo sya cingogho*

The *nembo sya cingogho* motif represents the shell of a turtle and constitutes, in the opinion of the majority of the decorators, the most attractive decorative motif. Due to its structure, it consumes rather a lot of time to produce it. For this reason, only a few of the decorators execute it.

It's construction is not very different from that of *nembo sya masweswe*: the motif *masweswe* is reflected horizontally (see Figure A.15).

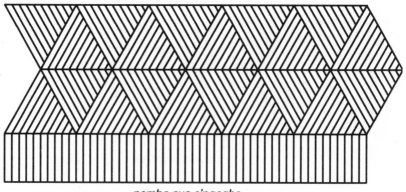

nembo sya cingogho
Figure A.15

6. *Nembo nguinyo kwinyo*

The *nembo nguinyo kwinyo* motif is inspired by a tattoo of the same name. This tattoo is made by incisions and is found on the cheek-bones. Like the parallel tattoo lines, the ceramic lines have the form of a fish-bone and may be drawn in several positions (see the examples in Figure A.16).

a

b 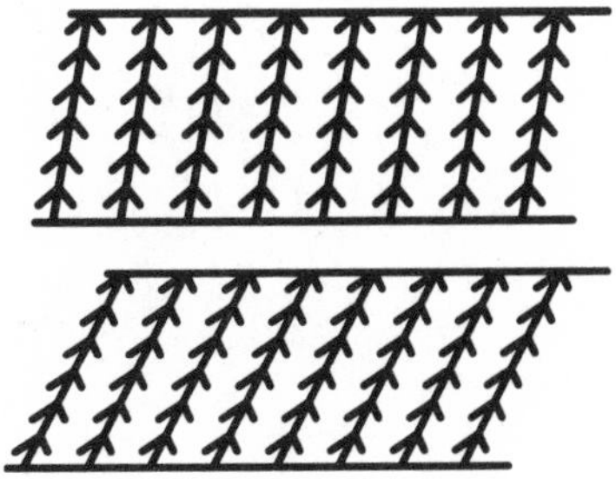
nembo nguinyo kwinyo
Figure A.16

According to Alaika Ali and Alaita Aidi, one obtains this decorative motif with a simple spatula of bamboo. One traces a group of equidistant oblique parallel lines *ndambala*. After this, one marks on each of the lines an equal number of equidistant L's of the same size.

7. *Nembo sya hitopfole*

The *nembo sya hitopfole* motif is also inspired by a tattoo of the same name. This tattoo is made by incisions in the form of a semicircle, in the space between the eyebrows, in the case of women, or on the arms, in the case of men. To do so one uses an iron instrument, that is called *nsondo* or *nguambo* which is in the form of a semicircle. Figure A.17 shows two ceramic decorations where the lower bands constitute the *nembo sya hitopfole* motif.

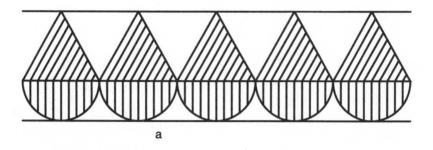

a

b

Figure A.17

Another variantion on ceramic pots is obtained by making in a single band from various rows of *hitopfole*, as in the example in Figure A.18.

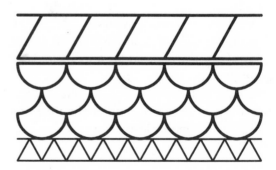

Figure A.18

The only difference for Alaita Aidi, that exists between the *hitopfole* on a face and the *hitopfole* impressed on a pot lies in its concavity. Where in ceramics the semicircles have their concavity directed upwards, those in tattoos are directed downwards, as the example in Figure A.19 illustrates. In the times of her grandmothers the *hitopfole* motif was never impressed on pots. She thinks that it were her 'mothers' who started to draw it on pots, when they stopped making tattoos.

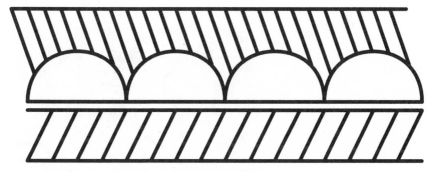

hitopfole in a tattoo
Figure A.19

8. *Nembo sya matipfa*

The *nembo sya matipfa* motif is also inspired by a tattoo of the same name. The tattoo was made with a sharp knife and with erotic intent. It was executed on the arms of men. This decorative motif is almost extinct. Only a few decorators use it. According to Alaika Ali, in the time when she learned to draw, people already showed little interest in this motif, although in the time of her grandmothers it constituted a highly valued motif. She further adds that it is possible that we are no longer capable of understanding its sensuality.

The motif consists of alternating groups of three to five oblique parallel lines. It is closed on the top and bottom by parallel lines (*lusiki - npumbulo*). Figure A.20 illustrates several variations.

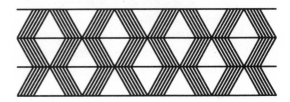

a1

a2
matipfa ga gona
a

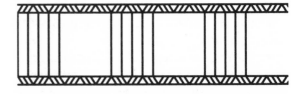

matipfa ga pingo
b
Figure A.20

9. *Nembo sya ditio*

Nembo sya ditio is, according to Alaita Aidi, one of the oldest motifs. It was abandoned a long time ago and she does not know why. It is still possible to encounter this motif in the areas where our ancestors lived, on the ceramic remains of that period.

When a woman is pregnant—Alaita explain—she prepares a special cord, called a *lusiki*. A spiral is made with the cord (*lukonji lwa kose kose*), which is fastened on the breasts or hips until child birth. The cord may only be unfastened during certain rituals. It was this spiral that gave the name to the decorative motif in ceramics. First one traces *ndambala* segments around a band of the pot. On each of these segments small *syungusya* ellipses are drawn which together give the impression of a spiral. The number of ellipses on each *ndambala* segment. Figure A.21 illustrates two examples.

a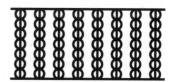

b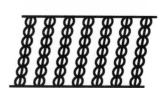
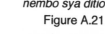
nembo sya ditio
Figure A.21

10. *Nembo sya njenjeleka*

The *nembo sya njenjeleka* motif (see Figure A.22) represents the situation, where a woman does not fulfill the prescribed rituals when unfastening the cord.

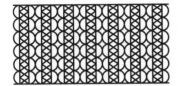

nembo sya njenjeleka
Figure A.22

11. *Nembo sya maguluka*

According to the potter Ambiti Chimbongue, the *nembo sya maguluka* motif (see Figure A.23) is impressed with an instrument made of gourd (*cipandingua can'gao*). It consists of a combination of the motifs *sya kusonda, masweswe* and *matipfa*. The vertical bands are obtained from horizontal ones by rotating them through a right angle. The word maguluka literally means "jumps".

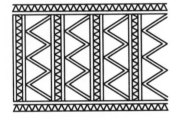

nembo sya maguluka
Figure A.23

12. *Nembo sya cinguku*

The potter Ambiti Chimbongue further explains that the *nembo sya cinguku* motif (see Figure A.24b) illustrates the behaviour of restless people who behave similar to chickens. The word *cinguku* means chicken, symbolised by the design in Figure A.24a.

cinguku - chicken
a

b

Figure A.24

13. *Nembo sya massamba*

In the Yao language *massamba* means leaf or figuratively all that may be easily lost. It is in this second sense that the potter Jenethy Kaisi transmits her message through the *nembo sya massamba* motif (see Figure A.25).

nembo sya massamba

Figure A.25

The measuring of the distance between two copies of the motif is done with a previously prepared instrument, generally either a spatula of bamboo or a toothed piece of gourd.

14. *Nembo sya nganhila*

The *nembo sya nganhila* motif (see Figure A.26) has a certain similarity with the *masweswe* motif. According to Jenethy Kaisi, this motif represents the growing up of a family head, from childhood to adulthood. During this time, the head does not return to its beginning, but a new chief emerges who fulfills the same itinerary. The word *nganhila* means growing-up.

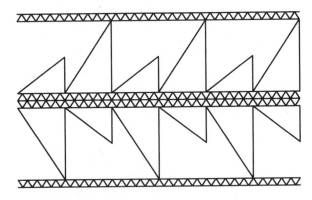

nembo sya nganhila
Figure A.26

15. *Nembo sya cingogho sya dikangala*

The *nembo sya cingogho sya dikangala* motif (Figure A.27b) has its origin in the *cingogho* (Figure A.27a) with the addition of *dikangala* which means mat. This motif symbolizes the rest of a chief. For Ambiti Chimbongue this motif transmits the value of the pots given to persons who are considered important in the cultural context.

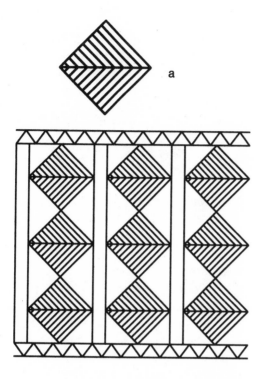

nembo sya cingogho sya dikangala
Figure A. 27

16. *Nembo sya madlassi sya miwa*

The decorative motif called *nembo sya madlassi sya miwa* (see Figure A.28) is, according to Ambiti Chimbongue, difficult to produce. It is a combination of the *lusondo* and *ndambala* motifs. The word *madlassi* indicates that it is with its black-and-white alternating similar to a chess board. The word *miwa* generally means cane, but symbolizes in this context richness or major production. According to Ambiti Chimbongue, this significance of this motif has died and only a few artisans know about it.

nembo sya madlassi sya miwa
Figure A.28

17. *Nembo sya dikangala sya usyausye*

To obtain the motif *nembo sya dikangala sya usyausye* (see Figure A.29b), one first traces a woven band (see Figure A.29a; cf. Figure A.14). Using a stone one then browns some parts of the "mat" thus generating the decorative strip. *Dikangala* literally means a place where one can sleep, represented by a woven bed.

a

nembo sya dikangala sya usyausye

b

Figure A.29

18. *Nembo sya maukouko*

Very similar to the *masweswe gasyun-gusya* and *hitopfole* motifs, is one called *nembo sya maukouko* (see Figure A.30a).

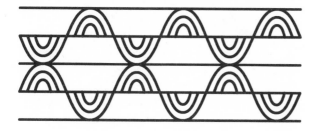

a

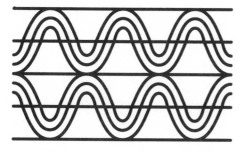

b

nembo sya maukouko

Figure A.30

It is obtained by the combination of these two motifs. The motif is impressed with the *nguambo* instrument and equal copies of it are produced by translating and reflecting the first imprint. According to Ambiti Chimbongue it is possible to join copies of the motif in such a way that continuous lines appear (see Figure A.30b). For her *maukouko* describes the imprint left in the sand by a lying body, either from an animal or from a person. The motif symbolizes laziness or the movements of a person who does nothing else but sit around.

Salimo Saide, June 1996

CLASSIFICATION OF STRIP PATTERNS

On the basis of the symmetries (one-colour) strip patterns have, one can classify them into seven (distinct) classes:

1. Strip patterns that simultaneously have vertical, horizontal, and 180° rotational symmetries;

2. Strip patterns that simultaneously have vertical, translational-reflected, and 180° rotational symmetries;

3. Strip patterns that have only vertical symmetry;

4. Strip patterns that have only horizontal symmetry;

5. Strip patterns that have only rotational symmetry of 180°.

6. Strip patterns that are invariant only under glide reflection (or reflected translation);

7. Strip patterns that are invariant only under translation and that have no other symmetry.

Table 1 contains a list of the seven possible classes, along with the characteristics of each class.

	Notation	Symmetries	Invariant under
1	*pmm2*	vertical, horizontal and rotational symmetry of 180°	vertical reflection, horizontal reflection and rotation through an angle of 180°
2	*pma2*	vertical, translational-reflected and rotational symmetry of 180°	vertical reflection, glide reflection and rotation through an angle of 180°
3	*pm11*	vertical symmetry	vertical reflection
4	*p1m1*	horizontal symmetry	horizontal reflection
5	*p112*	rotational symmetry of 180°	rotation through an angle of 180°
6	*p1a1*	translational-reflected symmetry	glide reflection (or reflected translation)
7	*p111*	only translational symmetry	only translation

Table 1

The second column gives the international notation for each class. In the third column, we do not indicate that all strip patterns have translational symmetry by definition.

In international notation, four symbols are used to represent each of the seven classes of strip patterns. The letter *p* denotes pattern. If the pattern has a vertical reflection, then the second symbol is *m* (of mirror); if not, then the second symbol is *1*. If the pattern is invariant under a horizontal reflection, then the third symbol will be *m*; if it is invariant under a glide reflection, then the third symbol is *a*; if it has neither a horizontal reflection nor a glide reflection, then the third symbol is *1*. The last symbol is *2*; if the pattern has 180° rotational symmetry (this symmetry is also called a symmetry of order 2); in all other circumstances, the last symbol is *1*.

For more information about (this and other) classifications of strip patterns (and plane patterns), the books by Washburn & Crowe and Grünbaum & Shephard are recommended.

REFERENCES

Abraham, A. Johnston, *String Figures* only translation, Reference Publications, Algonac Mi, 1988, 154 pp.

Amaral, Manuel Gama, *O povo Yao: subsídios para o estudo de um povo do noroeste de Moçambique* (1968), Instituto de Investigação Científica e tropical, Lisboa, 1990, 493 pp.

Ambrose, David, *The guide to Lesotho*, Winchester Press, Johannesburg & Maseru, 1976 (2nd. ed), 370 pp.

Assié-Lumumba, N'dri Thérése, *Demand, Access and Equity issues in African Higher Education*, Background paper for the Joint Colloquium on the University in Africa in the 1990's and beyond, Association of African Universities, Lesotho, 1995, 41 pp.

Ascher, Marcia *Ethnomathematics: a multicultural view of mathematical ideas*, Brooks/Cole Publishing Company, New York, 1991, 203 pp

Bannister, Anthony, *The Bushmen*, Struik, Cape Town, 1987, 24 pp.

Bannister, Anthony & Lewis-Williams, David, *Bushmen, a changing way of life*, Struik, Cape Town, 1991, 80 pp.

Baumann, Hermann, Afrikanisches Kunstgewerbe, in: H. Bossert (Ed.), *Geschichte des Kunstgewerbes aller Zeiten und Völker*, Berlin, Vol. 2, 1929, 51-148

Bishop, Alan, *Mathematical enculturation, a cultural perspective on mathematics education*, Kluwer Academic Publishers, Dordrecht, 1988, 195 pp.

Bishop, Alan (editor) *Mathematics Education and Culture*, Kluwer Academic Publishers, Dordrecht, 1988, 171 pp.

Bossert, Helmuth, *Folk art of Asia, Africa, Australia and the Americas*, Wasmuth, Tübingen, 1990 [reprint]

Carey, Margret, *Beads and beadwork of East and Southern Africa*, Shire, Bucks, 1986, 64 pp.

Casalis, Eugène, *The Basutos, twenty-three years in South Africa*, James Nisbet, London, 1861 [reprinted, 1992, Morija Museum & Archives, Morija, Lesotho]

Changuion, Paul (photographs); Matthews, Tom & Changuion, Annice (text), *The African mural*, Struik, Cape Town & New Holland, London, 1989, 166 pp.

Courtney-Clarke, Margaret, *Ndebele, the art of an African*

tribe, Rizzoli, New York, 1986, 200 pp.

D'Ambrosio, Ubiratan, *Socio-cultural bases for mathematics education*, University of Campinas, Campinas, 1985

D'Ambrosio, Ubiratan, *Etnomatemática, arte ou técnica de explicar e conhecer*, Editora Ática, São Paulo, 1990, 88 pp.

Dias, Jorge & Dias, Margot, *Os Macondes de Moçambique, Vol. 2, Cultura material*, Junta de Investigações do Ultramar, Lisboa, 1964, 192 pp.

Doumbia, Salimata & Pil, J. C., *Les jeux de cauris*, CEDA & IRMA, Abidjan 1992, 74 pp.

Ellert, H., *The material culture of Zimbabwe*, Longman Zimbabwe, Harare, 1984, 133 pp.

Elliot, Aubrey, *The Ndebele, art and culture*, Struik, Cape Town, 1989, 24 pp.

Elliot, Aubrey, *Zulu, heritage of a nation*, Struik, Cape Town, 1991, 80 pp.

Esterman, Carlos, *Etnografia do Sudoeste de Angola*, Vol. 2: *Grupo étnico Nhaneca-Humbe*, Junta de Investigações do Ultramar, Lisboa, 1960 (2nd edition), 299 pp.

Gerards, Constantino, Costumes dos Macuas do Mêdo, Região de Namuno, Circunscrição de Montepuez, in: *Moçambique — Documentário trimestral*, Lourenço Marques, 1941, Vol. XXVIII, 5-20

Gerdes, Paulus, A widespread decorative motif and the Pythagorean Theorem, in: *For the Learning of Mathematics*, Montreal, Vol. 8, No. 1, 1988, 35-39

Gerdes, Paulus, Fivefold symmetry and (basket) weaving in various cultures, in: I. Hargittai (ed.), 1992a, 245-262

Gerdes, Paulus (ed.), *Who is who in Mathematics and Mathematics Education in Southern Africa*, SAMSA, Maputo, 1992, 63 pp. (with supplement in 1993)

Gerdes, Paulus, On Mathematics in the History of Sub-Saharan Africa, in: *Historia Mathematica*, New York, Vol. 21, 1994, 345-376

Gill, Stephen, *A short history of Lesotho, From the late stone age until the 1993 elections*, Morija Museum & Archives, Morija, Lesotho, 1993, 266 pp.

Grossert, J.W. *Zulu crafts*, Shuter & Shooter, Pietermaritzburg, 1978, 64 pp.

Grünbaum, Branko & Shephard, G., *Tilings and Patterns*,
Freeman and Co., New York, 1987, 700 pp.

Haddon, A., String Figures from South Africa, in: *Journal of
the Royal Anthropological Institute*, 1906, Vol. 36, 142-149

Hardy, G.H., *A Mathematician's Apology*, Cambridge
University Press, Cambridge, 1940 [reprint, 1979, 153
pp.]

Hargittai, Istvan (ed.), *Symmetry: Unifying Human
Understanding*, Pergamon Press, Oxford, 1986

Hargittai, Istvan (ed.), *Symmetry: Unifying Human
Understanding 2*, Pergamon Press, Oxford,1072 pp.

Hargittai, Istvan (ed.), *Fivefold Symmetry*, Worl Scientific,
Singapore, 1992, 561 pp.

Hargittai, Istvan (ed.), *Spiral Symmetry*, Worl Scientific,
Singapore, 1992, 449 pp.

Hauenstein, Alfred, *Examen de motifs décoratifs chez les
Ovimbundu et Tchokwe d'Angola*, Instituto de
Antropologia, Universidade de Coimbra, Coimbra, 1988,
85 pp.

Heintze, Beatrix, *Ethnographische Zeichnungen der Lwimbi /
Ngangela (Zentral-Angola)*, Franz Steiner verlag,
Wiesbaden, 1988, 138 pp.

Junod, Henri, *The life of a South African tribe*, 1912 [reprinted
by University Books, New York, 1962, 2 vol., 559 pp.+
660 pp.]

Ki-Zerbo, Joseph, *Educate or Perish: Africa's Impass and
Prospects*, UNESCO-UNICEF, Dakar / Abidjan, 1990, 109
pp.

Levinsohn, Rhoda, *Art and craft in Southern Africa*, Delta
Books, Craighall, 1984, 144 pp.

Makhubu, Lydia, The contribution of women to science in
Africa, in: *Science in Africa, Achievements and Prospects*,
American Association for the Advancement of Science,
Washington, 1991, 137-145

Medeiros, Eduardo, *Notas para o trabalho sobre as tatuagens*,
Instituto Superior Pedagógico, Maputo, 1989, 5 pp.
(mimeographed)

Medeiros, Eduardo, *Dossier dos trabalhos dos estudantes sobre
tatuagens* (unpublished manuscript)

Migdoll, Ivor, *Field guide to the butterflies of southern Africa*,

Struik, Cape Town, 1992, 256 pp.

Milheiros, Mário, *Anatomia social dos Maiacas*, O Postulado, Luanda, 1956

Morris, Jean & Levitas, Ben, *South African tribal life today*, College Press, Cape Town, 160 pp.

Mothibe, B., *Litema designs collected by students at the National Teacher Training College of Lesotho*, NTTC Press, Maseru, 1976, 17 pp.

Njock, G., Mathématiques et environnement socio-culturel en Afrique Noire, in: *Présence Africaine*, 1985, Vol. 135, 3-21

Nyerere, Julius (ed.), *The challenge to the South*, Oxford University Press, Oxford, 1990, 325 pp.

Stewart, Ian & Golubitsky, Martin, *Fearful symmetry — Is God a geometer?*, Penguin, London, 1993, 287 pp.

UNESCO, *African Thoughts on the Prospects of Education for All*, UNESCO / UNICEF, Dakar / Abidjan, 1990, 193 pp.

Washburn, Dorothy & Crowe, Donald, *Symmetries of Culture: Theory and Practice of Plane Pattern Analysis*, University of Washington, Seattle, 1988, 300 pp.

Wedgwood, C. & Schapera, I., String figures from Bechuanaland Proctectorate, in: *Bantu Studies*, 1930, Vol.4, 251-268

West, Martin & Morris, Jean, *Abantu, an introduction to the black people of South Africa*, Struik, Cape Town, 1976, 184 pp.

Weyl, Hermann, *Symmetry* (1952), Princeton University Press, Princeton, 1989, 168 pp.

Williams, Geoffrey, *African designs from traditional sources*, Dover, New York, 1971, 200 pp.

Zaslavsky, Claudia, *Africa Counts: number and pattern in African culture*, 1973, Prindle, Weber and Schmidt, Boston, 328 pp. Paperback edition 1979: Lawrence Hill Books, Brooklyn.

SOURCES OF ILLUSTRATIONS

With the exception of Figures 4.1, 7.18, 8.11, A.1, A.2, and A.13 all drawings are by the author.

A. Figures

1.1 - 1.10 Author's drawings
2.1 - 2.12 New drawings. Author's collection.
3.1 - 3.3 Drawn after Morris & Levitas, photograph 164
4.1 Drawn after Junod, p. 174
5.1 Drawn after Estermann, p. 199, Ellert, p. 106
5.2 Author's collection
5.3 Drawn after Estermann, p. 199
5.4 Drawn after Heintze, Figures 73, 77, 79, 75, 74
5.5 Drawn after Milheiros, p. 272, 332
5.6 Drawn after Ellert, p. 93, 100, 106
5.7 Drawn after Morris & Levitas, photograph 120
5.8 Drawn after Amaral, p. 308
5.9 Drawn after Dias & Dias, p. 113, 115
5.10 Author's collection
5.11 Author's collection
6.1 - 6.5 New drawings. Author's collection
7.1 Drawn after Amaral, p. 309
7.2 Drawn after Amaral, p. 310
7.3 Drawn after Amaral, p. 312
7.4 New drawing
7.5 New drawing
7.6 Drawn after Suzana Raimundo, student's paper, 1993, Dossier of Eduardo Medeiros
7.7 Drawn after Adriano Niquice, student's paper, 1992, Dossier of Eduardo Medeiros
7.8 New drawing
7.9 Drawn after Adriano Niquice, student's paper, 1992, Dossier of Eduardo Medeiros
7.10 Drawn after Adriano Niquice, student's paper, 1992, Dossier of Eduardo Medeiros
7.11 Drawn after Alfredo Mecupe, student's paper, 1993, Dossier of Eduardo Medeiros
7.12 Drawn after Alfredo Mecupe, student's paper, 1993,

238

Dossier of Eduardo Medeiros

7.13 Drawn after Gerards, p. 8

7.14 Drawn after Gerards, p. 8

7.15 New drawing

7.16 Drawn after Gerards, p. 8

7.17 New drawing

7.18 Drawn after Heintze, p. 120

8.1 New drawing

8.2 Drawn after Hauenstein, p. 40, 50, 52, 53, 62

8.3 Drawn after Hauenstein, p. 63, 64, 66, 72, 73, 69

8.4 Drawn after Bossert, Table 9, photographs 5 and 12

8.5 Drawn after Bossert, Table 9, photographs 9 and 11

8.6 Drawn after Baumann, p.73, photograph 5

8.7 Drawn after Carey, p. 29, photograph 21

8.8 Drawn after Carey, p. 29, photograph 21

8.9 Drawn after Baumann, p.73, photographs 9 and 10

8.10 Drawn after Elliot, 1989, p.22, photograph 2; Courtney-Clarke, photograph on p. 90

8.11 Reproduced from Grossert, p. 54

8.12 Drawn after Elliot, 1991, p. 64, 65

8.13 Drawn after Morris & Levitas, photograph 56

8.14 - 8.18 New drawings. Author's collection

8.19 Drawn after Bannister & Williams, photographs on p. 75, 70, 25, 17

8.20 Drawn after Bannister & Williams, photograph on p. 12; Bannister, photographs on p. 3, 15

8.21 Drawn after Unicef postcards no. 502-E and no. 515-E

8.22 Drawn after Unicef postcard no. 501-E

8.23 Drawn after Williams, p. 61

8.24 Drawn after Carey, p. 59, photograph 40

9.1 Drawn after Mothibe, p. 10

9.2 Drawn after Changuion, photograph on p. 35

9.3 Drawn after Changuion, photograph on p. 134; Levinsohn, photograph on p. 28

9.4 Drawn after Mothibe, p. 9

9.5 Drawn after Mothibe, p. 8

9.6 Drawn after Mothibe, p. 7

9.7 Drawn after Mothibe, p. 13

9.8 Drawn after Mothibe, p. 13

9.9 Drawn after West & Morris, photograph 166

9.10 New drawing

9.11 Drawn after Mothibe, p. 8

9.12 Drawn after Mothibe, p. 3

9.13 Drawn after Mothibe, p. 9

9.14 Drawn after Mothibe, p. 6

9.15 Drawn after postcard from Visual Publications, Thaba Nchu, Lesotho

9.16 Drawn after Mothibe, p. 16

9.17 Drawn after Mothibe, p. 15

9.18 Drawn after Mothibe, p. 12

9.19 Drawn after Mothibe, p. 4

9.20 Drawn after Mothibe, p. 11

9.21 Drawn after Mothibe, p. 5

9.22 Drawn after Mothibe, p. 5

9.23 Drawn after Mothibe, p. 7

9.24 Drawn after Mothibe, p. 11

9.25 Drawn after Mothibe, p. 15

9.26 Drawn after Mothibe, p. 4

9.27 - 9.35   New drawings

9.36 Drawn after Changuion, photograph on p. 123

9.37 Drawn after Changuion, photograph on p. 106

9.38 Drawn after Changuion, photograph on p. 13

9.39 Drawn after Changuion, photograph on p. 110

9.40 Drawn after Changuion, photograph on p. 119

9.41 Drawn after Changuion, photograph on p. 12

9.42 Drawn after Changuion, photograph on p. 116

9.43 Drawn after Changuion, photograph on p. 105

9.44 Drawn after Changuion, photograph on p. 66

9.45 Drawn after Changuion, photograph on p. 151

9.46 Drawn after Levinsohn, photograph on p. 27

9.47 Drawn after Changuion, photograph on p. 104

9.48 Drawn after Changuion, photograph on p. 6 (cf. photograph on p. 115, Sotho, North-eastern Free State)

9.49 Drawn after Changuion, photograph on p. 117

9.50 Drawn after Changuion, photograph on p. 125

9.51 Drawn after Changuion, photograph on p. 124

9.52 - 9.59 New drawings

9.60 Drawn after Changuion, photograph on p. 124, 125

10.1 Drawn after Levinsohn, photograph on p. 127

10.2 Drawn after Elliot, 1989, p. 11, photograph 7

10.3 New drawing

10.4 Drawn after Courtney-Clarke, photograph on p. 47

10.5 Drawn after Courtney-Clarke, photograph on p. 69

10.6 Drawn after Courtney-Clarke, photograph on p. 76

10.7 Drawn after Courtney-Clarke, photograph on p. 164

10.8 New drawing

10.9 Drawn after Courtney-Clarke, photograph on p. 151

10.10 New drawing

10.11 Drawn after Elliot, 1989, photographs on p. 12 and 17; Courtney-Clarke, photographs on p. 170, 170, and 63

10.12 New drawing

10.13 Drawn after Morris & Levitas, photograph 35

11.1 Drawn after Hauenstein, p. 42

11.2 Drawn after Hauenstein, p. 61

11.3 Drawn after Hauenstein, p. 69

11.4 Drawn after Hauenstein, p. 71

11.5 Drawn after Hauenstein, p. 73

11.6 Drawn after Hauenstein, p. 54

11.7 Drawn after Hauenstein, p. 57, 56

11.8 Drawn after Hauenstein, p. 64

11.9 - 11.13 Author's drawings

A.1 - A.2 Drawings by Marcos Cherinda after sketches by Salimo Saide

A.3 - A.12 Drawn after sketches by Salimo Saide

A.13 Drawing by Marcos Cherinda after sketch by Salimo Saide

A.14 - A.30 Drawn after sketches by Salimo Saide

B. Photographs

1.1, 1.2, 2.1, 2.2, 6.1, 8.1   Marcos Cherinda (UP)

10.1 Walter Knirr (Postcard Constantia Greeting Ltd.), photograph taken at Ndebele Open Air Museum, Botshebelo, South Africa

BOOKS BY THE SAME AUTHOR

On the awakening of geometrical thinking:

* *Ethnogeometrie. Kulturanthropologische Beiträge zur Genese und Didaktik der Geometrie* [Ethnogeometry: Cultural anthropological contributions to the Genesis and Didactics of geometry], Verlag Franzbecker, Bad Salzdetfurth, 1990, 360 pp. [preface by Prof. Peter Damerow]
* *Cultura e o Despertar do Pensamento Geométrico* [Culture and the Awakening of Geometrical Thinking], Universidade Pedagógica (UP), Maputo, 1992, 146 pp.
* *Sobre o despertar do pensamento geométrico* [On the Awakening of Geometrical Thinking], Federal University of Paraná, Curitiba [Brazil], 1992, 105 pp. [preface by Prof. Ubiratan D'Ambrósio]

On the sand drawing tradition and its use in education and mathematics:

* *Vivendo a matematica: desenhos da África* [Living Mathematics: Drawings from Africa], Editora Scipione, São Paulo [Brazil], 1990, 68 pp. (3rd edition 1994) [Alba Mahan Prize 1990]
* *Lusona: Geometrical recreations of Africa / Recréations géométriques d'Afrique*, African Mathematical Union & UP, Maputo, 1991, 118 pp. [preface by Prof. Aderemi Kuku].
  New edition by: L'Harmattan, Paris / Montreal, 1997, 127 pp.
* *Sona Geometry: Reflections on the sand drawing tradition of peoples of Africa south of the Equator*, UP, Maputo, 1994, Vol.1, 200 pp. [translation from the Portuguese by A.Powell]
* *Une tradition géométrique en Afrique. — Les dessins sur le sable* [A Geometrical Tradition in Africa – The Sand Drawings], L'Harmattan, Paris, 1995, Vol. 1: *Analyse et reconstruction*, 247 pp.; Vol. 2: *Exploration éducative et mathématique*, 184 pp.; Vol. 3: *Analyse comparative*, 144 pp. [originally published in Portuguese]
* *Lunda Geometry — Designs, Polyominoes, Patterns,*

242

Symmetries, UP, Maputo, 1996, 149 pp.
* *Ethnomathematik am Beispiel der Sonageometrie in Afrika,* Spektrum Verlag, Berlin, 1997, 436 pp.

On ethnomathematics as a field of research:
* *Etnomatemática: Cultura, Matemática, Educação,* UP, Maputo, 1992, 115 pp. [preface by Prof. Ubiratan D'Ambrosio]
* *Ethnomathematics and Education in Africa,* University of Stockholm, 1995, 184 pp.
* *L'ethnomathématique comme nouveau domaine de recherche en Afrique: quelques réflexions et experiences du Mozambique,* UP, Maputo, 1993, 84 pp.

Other ethnomathematical studies
* *Sipatsi: Technology, Art and Geometry in Inhambane* (co-author Gildo Bulafo), UP, Maputo, 1994, 102 pp. [also published in French and Portuguese]
* *African Pythagoras: A study in Culture and Mathematics Education,* UP, Maputo, 1994, 103 pp. [also published in Portuguese]
* (editor) *A numeração em Moçambique: Contribuição para uma reflexão sobre cultura, língua e educação matemática* [Numeration in Mozambique: Contribution to a Reflection on Culture, Language and Mathematics Education], UP, Maputo, 1993, 159 pp.
(editor)*Explorations in Ethnomathematics and Ethnoscience in Mozambique,* UP, Maputo, 1994, 76 pp.

On mathematics, education, and society:
* *Mathematics, Education and Society* (co-editors C.Keitel, A.Bishop, P.Damerow), Science and Technology Education Document Series No. 35, UNESCO, Paris, 1989, 193 pp.

"Women and Geometry in Southern Africa" is also published in French:
* *Femmes et Géométrie en Afrique Australe,* L'Harmattan, Paris / Montreal, 1996, 219 pp.

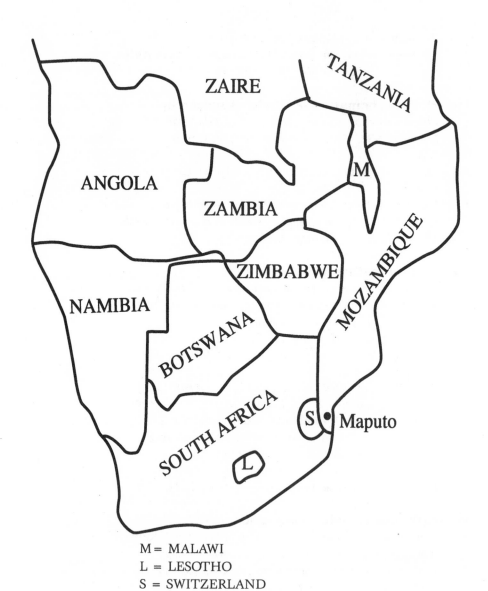

M = MALAWI
L = LESOTHO
S = SWITZERLAND